BANDIDO

BOOKS IN ENGLISH BY ILAN STAVANS

NONFICTION

Bandido: Oscar "Zeta" Acosta and the Chicano Experience

The Hispanic Condition:
Reflections on Culture and Identity in America

Imagining Columbus: The Literary Voyage

ANTHOLOGIES

Tropical Synagogues:
Short Stories by Jewish Latin American Writers

Growing Up Latino: Memoirs and Stories
(co-edited with Harold Augenbraum)

TRANSLATION

Sentimental Songs
by Felipe Alfau

BANDIDO

Oscar "Zeta" Acosta and the Chicano Experience

ILAN STAVANS

IconEditions
An Imprint of HarperCollins*Publishers*

HarperCollins books may be purchased for educational, business, or sales promotional use. For information please write: Special Markets Department, HarperCollins Publishers, Inc., 10 East 53rd Street, New York, NY 10022.

FIRST EDITION

Designed by Alma Hochhauser Orenstein

Library of Congress Cataloging-in-Publication Data

Stavans, Ilan.
  Bandido : Oscar "Zeta" Acosta & the Chicano experience / Ilan Stavans. — 1st ed.
    p. cm.
  Includes bibliographical references and index.
  ISBN 0-06-438557-4
  1. Acosta, Oscar Zeta. 2. Mexican Americans—West (U.S.)—Biography. 3. Mexican Americans—West (U.S.)—Ethnic identity. 4. West (U.S.)—Biography. I. Title.
CT275.A186S73   1995
978'.0046872073'0092—dc20
[B]   95-21741

95 96 97 98 99 ❖/HC 10 9 8 7 6 5 4 3 2 1

For Rolando Hinojosa-Smith

For by death is wrought greater change than hath been shown. Whereas in general the spirit that removed cometh back upon occasion, and is sometimes seen of those in flesh (appearing in the form of the body it bore) yet it hath happened that the veritable body without the spirit hath walked. And it is attested of those encountering who have lived to speak thereon that a lich so raised up hath no natural affection, nor remembrance thereof, but only hate. Also, it is known that some spirits which in life were benign become by death evil altogether.

RIDWAN IBN ALI

CONTENTS

ACKNOWLEDGMENTS

I wish to thank Marco Acosta for his friendship and for permission to quote from Oscar Acosta's unpublished material at the library of the University of California, Santa Barbara, as well as from *The Autobiography of a Brown Buffalo* and *The Revolt of the Cockroach People,* reprinted by Vintage in 1989. Mr. Acosta was an invaluable help throughout my research, answering questions and guiding my attention and interests. His mother, Betty Daves, and his aunt Anita Acosta also offered invaluable responses. Thanks also to Salvador Güereña, director of the Colección Cloque Nahuaque at the UCSB library, without whose help and friendship I would have been unable to track down innumerable sources, and to Denise Fullbrook at Houghton Mifflin, who inspired me to write this essay. Thanks to Rolando Hinojosa-Smith, José Agustín, Sandra Cisneros, Trinidad Sánchez, Jr., Manuel Ramos, Raúl R. Salinas, Martín Espada, John Bruce-Novoa, Rudolfo Anaya, and Tomás Ybarra-Frausto for their guidance and for answering my questions, often at unlikely hours.

Thanks to the countless people, famous and otherwise, I talked to about Acosta, whose response are the quilt behind my views. Thanks to Hunter S. Thompson for keeping Acosta's mythological stature alive. Finally, thanks to my dear friend Harold Augenbraum, with whom I first embarked in the enchanting journey of Chicano literature and culture and whose Virgil presence is simply invaluable. Other people also offered me light and encouragement: Marc Jaffe, Liz T. Fowler, Robin Desser at Vintage International, Scott Vickers and Marilyn Auer at *The Bloomsbury Review,* Henry Finder at *The New Yorker,* Mike Vasquez at *Transition,* as well as Cass Canfield, Jr., and Karen Shapiro at HarperCollins.

BANDIDO

VANISHING ACT

Excess. Nothing works like excess. A few surviving photographs, part of a portfolio of Annie Leibovitz, show him as a Tennessee Williams type. He's obese, barefooted, dark skinned, and angry—in today's world, an all-American character, at once extravagant and immoderate. His pants are baggy, his hair jumbled, his belt overused, his thumbs inside his pockets, his facial gesture openly defiant. He personifies a proto-*mestizo*, what the early twentieth-century Mexican thinker and educator José Vasconcelos envisioned, in Nietzschean terms, as *el superhombre de bronce*: a Bronze Superman. Somehow he reminds me of Stanley Kowalski in *A Streetcar Named Desire*, as played by Marlon Brando. A Stanley looking for his southern belle, his Blanche du Bois. A dynamic, vibrant Stanley, annoyed by pretensions of gentility. A flirtatious yet angry Stanley. Zeta is in his undershirt, elegant suit pants, excited but probably a bit worried about his ulcers, with pronounced lines in his forehead. He is thirty-eight. Although worn out, he still champions a mysterious aura. *¡Qué cábula!* What a crazy dude, a *vato loco!* He is finally ready to put away his ghost-like identity to emerge as a recognized name in mainstream culture, a desire he has nourished for decades. It's 1972, and once the photo study by Leibovitz—whom Zeta would call, in his résumé and in brief bios, not without a hint of pretentiousness, "my official photographer"—has been taken, he will wait impatiently. Metaphorically, Leibovitz's lens is a mirror in front of which Zeta stands naked, con- templating the deterioration of his physical self. Has his life been plentiful? Does his entire existential journey make any sense? Has he made the most of his *yo mexicano,* his inner, south-of-the-border self? How has he been able to reconcile his rambunctious past with the future he hopes to achieve? How many more days are left in his private calen- dar? How many more LSD trips will he undergo? And where is he going now? He will survive only a couple of years more, no more. Nobody will be sure about his final fate. He will be involved in drug trafficking, and during a trip on a friend's boat, in June 1974, from Mazatlán, a resort place on Mexico's Pacific coast, to Southern California, he will disappear, strangely and without trace. (The back cover of the 1989 paperback edition of his two published books mistakenly claim his death year to be 1971.) A *desapare- cido.* Is he still *entre nosotros,* alive somewhere in the hemisphere? Maybe. Rumors surrounding his vanishing act, his big sleep, never stop. Some claim Zeta might have died of a drug overdose. Too much cocaine. Or too much LSD. Excess in excess. The very last we know about him is from a long-distance phone call on May 15, 1974, at around 6:30 P.M., to his beloved son, Marco Acosta, now a lawyer and guitar player in San Francisco, who attended St. John's College at Annapolis, Maryland, and is Zeta's sole literary executor. Marco was fifteen years old at the time. "I was the last person, as far as I know, to speak with him," he told me during an interview. "Moments before he got on the boat in which he was planning to ride back to the United States, I told him I hoped he knew what he was doing. He said he hoped *I* knew what I was doing with my life." Zeta also insinuated he was swimming in a pool of white powder. White dust. A bed of snow. Cocaine.

"Let's face it," his friend Hunter S. Thompson once wrote in a requiem, "you [Zeta] were not real light on your feet in this world, and you were too goddamn heavy for most of the boats you jumped into." Betty Daves, his first wife, who since their divorce in 1963 has remarried and lives in San Francisco not far from her son, Marco, suggested to me that Zeta's disappearance ought to be read as a Henry James novel: open, unsolved, indecipherable. "That's exactly how he wished to be remembered: as a ghost with an ambiguous edge," she claimed when we talked over the phone. "He was touchingly dear, a charmer, a man of immense talents. He could get a job in any field he pleased. Once he even worked as a chemist and a pharmacist in St. Louis. But he was a victim of a merciless racist society, a product of abysmal differences between people. And he lived to personify that victimhood like no one else. Where is he now? I don't know. Nobody does. We aren't allowed to know. He might have gone to help Fidel Castro. He might be imprisoned in a Guatemalan jail. He might even be in Nicaragua, collaborating with Daniel Ortega and the Sandinistas. . . . While alive, he was an enigma. And that, as it stands, is his best legacy." In other words, only in death did he find satisfaction. It's better for us not to know. Better to remain enchanted with Zeta the riddle. A riddle wrapped in a mystery inside an enigma.

While Leibovitz is doing her work, he recapitulates. He ponders his achievements. He analyzes his legal and political careers. Life sometimes seems infinite, but he has reached the age when he knows it isn't. Things must come to an end. They carry within themselves their own conclusion—their own death. How many more joints will he smoke? Identification: Oscar Acosta, also known as the Brown Z. Buffalo; Mexican-American male; height: six feet one; weight: 225 pounds; hair: black; eyes: brown; occupation: attorney, hyphen, writer; Social Security number: 552-42-0164. The man is only allowed a total of, say, forty summers, a couple of failed marriages, 502 violent outbursts, eight arrests, 9,702 Dos Equis, 12,301 cups of coffee, 103 guacamole appetizers, 3,401 tequilas straight up, seven automobiles. . . . Numbers, numbers, life is always about numbers, and death, as the American expatriate Paul Bowles wrote in *The Sheltering Sky,* is always on the way. "The fact that you don't know when it will arrive seems to take away from the fineness of life. It's that terrible precision that we hate so much. But because we don't know, we get to think of life as an inexhaustible well." Whenever Death (with capital *D*) takes him *de acá,* Zeta is sure a record of his odyssey will be available for the next generation of *La Raza.*

A mythical aura already surrounds him. A couple of

years before, as Zeta's 1970 campaign for sheriff of Los Angeles County was in high gear, Anthony Quinn, at a public gathering in Los Angeles, claimed that Zeta's ultimate impact would be transgenerational. And of course he was right. Zeta was a man ahead of his time, a Chicano for the future. He understood that identity and ethnicity would sooner or later become mainstream concerns in the United States. *Raza e identidad.* In his autobiography, he wrote: "For twelve years, all through college and law school, I'd been unable to get rid of any printed or written material that in any way whatsoever touched me. I'd kept all my text books, my exams, my notes, schedules of classes, announcements of events, hungry poems written in the dark on scraps of paper, and any other paraphernalia that described me. I was going to make certain that my biographers had all the information they'd need to make a complete report." Immortality—Zeta didn't want to achieve it through his work but through his actions. He was self-conscious about his legendary stature, about his larger-than-life legacy. An abundance of drugs, sex, alcohol, relentless politics, and a confused, double-faceted, heterogeneous self—resistance and affirmation have been his motto.

He is the king of *rascuachismo, el rey* of low taste. A colloquialism ignored by the standard *Diccionario de la Real Academia Española, rascuache* is used in the streets of East Los Angeles to describe a cultural item of inferior quality, of proletarian origin. Zeta isn't kitschy, i.e., parodic, self-referential, inbred with intentional exaggeration, or perhaps misrepresentation, of human feelings. *Nunca,* no way. On the contrary. Zeta's pachuco style, his rough Stanley Kowalski mannerisms, seasoned with a *mexicano* flavor, are simply considered cheap, outside the demarcations of approved taste and decorum. He is, was, and always will be considered by the Anglo bourgeoisie as vulgar, inferior, undeserving, tasteless, of low quality. *Mestizo* and without hope. *Rascuache* is a sine qua non term to describe his idiosyncratic attitude. As Tomás Ybarra-Frausto, a Chicano critic, explains: "To be *rascuache* is to posit a bawdy, spunky consciousness, to seek to subvert and turn ruling paradigms upside down. It is a witty, irreverent, and impertinent posture that recodes and moves outside established boundaries." In Zeta's environment, the Chicano community of the Southwest, his demeanor becomes something of an insider private code. "Very generally," Ybarra-Frausto argues further, "*rascuachismo* is an underdog perspective— a view from *los de abajo,* an attitude rooted in resourcefulness and adaptability, yet mindful of stance and style. . . . It presupposes the worldview of the have-nots, but is also a quality exemplified in objects and places (a *rascuache* car or restaurant) and in social comportment (a person who is or acts *rascuache*)." Ybarra-Frausto even distinguishes levels of *medio* and *muy,* low and high *rascuachismo*: Microwave tamales, shopping at Kmart, flour tortillas made with vegetable oil, pretending you are Spanish, and portraits of Emiliano Zapata on velvet slippers belong to the first category; to the second, flour tortillas made with lard, shopping at JCPenney, portraits of Francisco Villa on velvet slippers, and Cantinflas. In that scheme, Zeta is *muy pero muy rascuache*: the limit, an extreme. So *vato loco,* now's the time to go tell the Anglos *que se vayan pal' carajo!*

After an endless, emotionally consuming search for his

paternal figure, one that in some way mirrors Zeta's own journey, Marco Acosta donated his father's manuscripts, stored in several carton boxes, to a special collection at the library of University of California at Santa Barbara: love poems; legal documents; the FBI file number 170 617-B; letters to family and friends; unpublished sketches and short stories like "To Whom It May Concern," "The Worm Dieth Not," "The Little House," "From Whence I Came," "Eight for the Show," and "Waiting"; newspaper clippings; a 1964 letter to a certain Wendy that becomes an exercise in creative writing; academic essays by critics like John Bruce-Novoa, Raymund A. Paredes, Ramón Saldívar, Joe D. Rodríguez, et al.; an ill-conceived experimental play entitled *The Catalina Papers*; a fascinating sixty-minute, black-and-white unedited video of Zeta smoking marijuana while sitting next to his son and some acquaintances in somebody's kitchen; nonfiction material such as an autobiographical essay and a text on racial exclusion; a letter to the Chicano people drafted *en español*; a testament; and his declaration of candidacy to the job of sheriff of Los Angeles County. There's certainly no shortage of biographical and creative material. And yet, much remains lost. Lost or simply misplaced, including a novel Zeta wrote when he was around age thirty-three and which no publisher accepted and only one or two acknowledged receiving. I also found out that more biographical material was at the home of Zeta's late second wife, Socorro Aguiniga, who once or twice promised to donate it to her alma mater, the University of California at Los Angeles, but never found time to do so. Since her death in mid-1994, the whereabouts of her stuff remains unknown.

What could the most urgent item in need of clarification be if not his hybrid, convoluted identity? "He was a real sweetheart," said Harriet Fier, a switchboard secretary at *Rolling Stone* in the early seventies who rose to the position of managing editor. Her statement summarizes the perceptions most acquaintances had of Zeta. They all loved him, but they also loved to hate him. Most people I have talked to always claim his departure, and perhaps his entire life, was a waste. A waste of intellectual stamina. A waste of human energy. A waste of political vision. How could it not be? Much of the Hispanic experience in North America often seems to me that way: made of short-lived heroic impulses, aborted outbursts to overcome miserable circumstances. I see Zeta, not without reason, as a collective paradigm, a useful pattern, a metaphor of millions that are dissipated, without coherent and cohesive guidance. Millions, as Susan Ertz once put it, who long for immortality but don't know what to do with themselves on a rainy Sunday afternoon. That's why he was a careless guide for the unattended, a self-alienated schizoid who passed through life as the Son of God.

So there you have it: Zeta the genius; Zeta the real sweetheart; Zeta the revolutionary who stepped into history at the end of the sixties and then, when the world had no place for him anymore, temporarily disappeared. *Temporalmente*. After all, people cannot live in a constant state of revolution, and by the seventies, Zeta's calling was off. His journey, nevertheless, is a sine qua non in American history: an epoch-making life plagued by excess, a pilgrimage pushed to the very limit. Zeta: the last letter in the alphabet, the last zoot-suiter, our last LA rioter, our most beloved urban freedom fighter. He went from rejecting his ethnic ancestry to fighting for collective recognition and granting hope to the whole Chicano people of the Southwest. He knew he was an underground hero, an endearing outlaw, a *bandido*, and he thoroughly enjoyed the idea. Probably not quite a symbolic figure for the current generation, but those born before the chaotic Vietnam decade embraced his cause wholeheartedly. They would turn around if he was nearby, their Mexican-American Robin Hood, a reincarnation of Joaquín Murrieta, Tiburcio Vásquez, and Gregorio Cortez, all three notorious border bandits blended into one—the next Augusto César Sandino, a precursor of Subcomandante Marcos, a West Coast Ernesto "Ché" Guevara. Animosity, outspokenness, guts. He was carefully ambiguous about just about everything: politics, mental stability, loyalties. He turned friends into enemies and vice versa. He brought out the best and worst in people, hope and fury. Doubt, disbelief, distrust, hesitancy were his trademarks. *¡El diablo anda suelto!* The only thing he knew for sure and wanted others to be certain about was that the American Dream is really a nightmare—that good is evil, *el mal del bien.* More than anybody, he incarnated that nightmare. Paraphrasing the legendary Chicano theater director Luis Valdez, Zeta was the ultimate *hombre mucho mal.*

Click—Annie Leibovitz's snapshot is taken: Zeta is now immortal!

Z AND I

Not Oscar Acosta but Z—I'd rather address him simply as Zeta. By using the pseudonym he selected for himself, the mask he chose to use, I'm acknowledging his true identity. I'm making him mine, turning him not only into my object of biographical inquiry but, more particularly, into a facet of myself. Object and subject—Z, my *Zeta*, a mirror through which the whole Chicano experience, his and mine, ought to be understood.

I never met him, of course. At least not *cara a cara*. He disappeared when I was thirteen years old. I was born and raised in Mexico, and in spite of Zeta's Mexican ancestry nobody knows him or has ever heard of him south of the Tortilla Curtain. I recently asked José Agustín, a popular Mexican novelist who belongs to the *La Onda* generation of the sixties, the equivalent of the beatniks in the United States, if he had ever heard of Zeta. "No. Nunca. Para nada . . . ," he replied categorically. His anonymity *entre hermanos* is not surprising: Chicanos are often ignored in Mexico—after all, they betrayed the mother country. But he is also largely unknown in the English-speaking world, *su propio mundo*, his very own world.

I first read Zeta's work in early 1992, and my relationship with him has been, consequently, through the printed word. Bookish, intellectual. I came across his name shortly before editing an anthology of stories and memoirs. I read his two volumes, *The Autobiography of a Brown Buffalo* and *The Revolt of the Cockroach People*, and wanted something by him in my volume. (I ended up using chapter 6 of the former.) Time came to request permissions, and his publisher forwarded my letter to Marco Acosta. After a brief, friendly conversation, he mentioned the existence of boxes containing his father's manuscripts. A passionate reader of detective fiction, I traveled to California a couple of months later and slowly went through all the material. Some clues to Zeta's identity began to obsess me. Who was he? What was his true gift? I began talking to his people: family members, friends, acquaintances, and then to Latino novelists (among them, a couple of mystery writers such as Manuel Ramos), American historians, literary critics. At some point I remember deciding that the best way to understand him was to write about him, to turn his life into my narrative. *Escribo, luego existo.* Writing, Georges Simenon said, is not a profession but a vocation of unhappiness. And it is also a strategy to make coherent the incomprehensible. Ironically, this was the same road he chose after he quit defending poor Hispanics in East LA and was defeated in his campaign for sheriff of Los Angeles County: He opted for literature as a redeeming act, the written word as a way of knowledge and salvation.

The act of writing a biographical investigation is not unlike sleuthing. As one sets out to unravel the mysteries of a life distant, different from ours, traveling deeper into the field of detective work, the object of the search acquires a variety of shades and at times is made to resemble our own plight. The biographer first identifies with the biographee, gets to know him wholeheartedly, then detests his odyssey, what he represents, and finally settles for a critical respect through which his investigative text can emerge. Body snatching: In the end, one learns to live in and through somebody else's skin. "The concept of privacy," writes Janet Malcolm in *The Silent Woman,* "is a sort of screen to hide the fact that almost none is possible in a social universe. In any struggle between the public's inviolable right to be diverted and an individual's wish to be left alone, the public almost always prevails." Zeta is partly myself and vice versa. *Zeta c'est moi.* He embodies a Dr. Jekyll–and–Mr. Hyde division of self so appealing to me: part Anglo, part Hispanic; or better, fully American and, simultaneously, fully Mexican—*dos en uno,* two for the price of one. He is relentless in his self-search, a lonesome soul attempting to explain the abyss within all of us. Like a Borgesian creation, at some point he surely came to understand that the ultimate goal of his search was utterly meaningless. That the act of searching is an end in itself. He knew the abysmal wound dividing his psyche would never heal. He would be eternally unhappy, constantly angry and unfulfilled. *Desde siempre y para siempre.* But it mattered no more. His suffering could acquire meaning only through literature, through its written expression. Zeta has

now undergone a chemical metamorphosis: His impa-
tience, his fury, his anger, his obesity are *mías* and mine
alone.

It's better not to have known him. Better to imagine
who he was, to reinvent him. Writers tend to be unappeal-
ing creatures: arrogant, overbearing, presumptuous, self-
serving. Better to have come too late to witness his embar-
rassing Epicurean performance on earth. Zeta spent his
life making a fool of himself. He enjoyed being repulsive. I
probably would have disliked his physical presence. The
photographs I've seen of him—next to his father, sharing a
table with Hunter S. Thompson—are unequivocal: He was
the embodiment of what I've tried repeatedly to leave out
of my life: the cult of the body, life as a bohemian trip
through altered states of consciousness, one's own behavior as a lousy imitation of a Carlos Castañeda mystical
imbroglio: spaced out, disoriented, a space cadet with a
passion for villainy. His tics are an open encyclopedia of
sixties *Chicanismo*. Who else but him to champion a vision
of victory through repulsion?

Excess: The word comes back to me. Zeta was redun-
dant, extravagant, and immoderate. What I detest in him is
obviously what I'm most afraid of in myself: excess in politics, excess of self-pity, excess of self-glory. He is an
immoralist, a hedonist, a ferocious beast trapped in the
skin of a Mexican-American. He is mysterious and he fasci-
nates me because, in some metaphysical way, I often
secretly dream of vanishing. *Desvanecerme sin rastro*. Forever and without a trace. And I dream of assuming a new,
altogether different identity. Zeta, in my eyes, means fear

and courage. Fear and violence. Fear and authenticity. Fear and loathing. Devastating fear. Enigmatic fear. Unmerciful fear and never-ending loathing of Anglo-Saxon treasures.

Is his inconclusive end a prophecy? Somehow I've come to endorse this thesis. The many enemies he accumulated while a legal aid lawyer in Los Angeles might have hired a killer to delete him from the face of the globe. He could have had a nervous breakdown, losing control of his behavior. Or perhaps he ended up the victim of foul play, a hypothesis ventured by a handful of Chicano acquaintances. In fact, some people believe that the FBI may even have been involved in his disappearance. Too outrageous. Too perverse. *Un hijo de puta.* Hunter Thompson, an acolyte and the author of *Fear and Loathing in Las Vegas,* who is well known, as critic John Bruce-Novoa rightly puts it, as a passionate supporter of the American Dream, "a believer in America as the land of opportunity and tolerance," which sometimes makes him experience "bitterness about the distortion the Dream has suffered, about what that term has come to signify," is among many when he speculates, in a reminiscence published in *Rolling Stone* magazine in December 1977, about the reasons as to why Zeta vanished, never to reappear. He suffered terrible doubts about his masculinity, Thompson claims, bouts of paranoia, and a relentless fear of being driven mad by society. "Oscar was a wild boy. He stomped on any terra he wandered into, and many people feared him. . . . His birthday is not noted in any calendar, and his death was barely noticed. . . . But the hole that he left was a big one, and nobody even tried to sew it up. He was a player. He was Big. And when he roared into your driveway at night, you knew he was bringing music, whether you wanted it or not. . . . I have never liked writing about him, because it makes me think too much, and I can never find the right words to explain the terrible joy that he brought with him wherever he went. . . . You had to be there, I guess, and you had to understand that the man was never comfortable unless he was in the company of people who were crazier than he was."

Crazy and bellicose. His aggressions still hurt. A noted critic once described him as "a startlingly bizarre character . . . in an era when eccentrics languished on park benches in every medium-size American city." While interviewing family members, friends, and acquaintances, I came across a poet who argued that Zeta had survived an assassination attack and is alive and well, hiding in a cave near Cuernavaca, next to Emiliano Zapata, the revered desperado and rural soldier in the Mexican Revolution who, according to a campesino version, was not killed in 1919, betrayed by Colonel Jesús Guajardo, but survived. He sent an impostor to die in his place. He's alive and well, somewhere. Anywhere and everywhere. Consummate actors, Zapata and Zeta, the two Zs, share the same cavern in the southern Mexican state of Oaxaca. Or in Morelos, where men are *muy machos*. Or perhaps in Chiapas. From there they continue to support freedom fighters world-wide, from Nicaragua to El Salvador, from Angola to Afghanistan. Who knows? Even "Ché" Guevara, suppos-edly killed in Bolivia in 1967 but still undead, might also be sharing the shelter. *Los tres amigos*. The cave of *los bandi-dos inmortales*.

Even Zeta's son at times seems to support such an outrageous thesis. In the January 1989 afterword to his father's two novels, he suggests "the fantastic possibility that he's alive on some island planning the next revolution." "Yeah, that's him folks," Thompson adds affectionately. "My boy, my brother, my partner in too many crimes. Oscar Zeta Acosta. Stand back. He is gone now, but even his memory stirs up wind that will blow heavy cars off the road. He was a monster, a true child of the century—faster than Bo Jackson and crazier than Neal Cassady. . . . When the Brown Buffalo disappeared, we all lost one of those high notes that we will never hear again. Oscar was one of God's own prototypes—a high-powered mutant of some kind who was never even considered for mass production. He was too weird to live and too rare to die."

Yeah, yeah. To be perfectly honest, Zeta's life after life, his vitae post mortem, seems to me even more compelling than his amazing odyssey on earth. Death, indeed, revealed the eminent in him. He has entered the hall of larger-than-life entities whose magnetism and mystical power serve as inspiration for revolt and change. In Chicano campus revolts in the eighties and onward, his image has served as instigator. He is a stimulus among Chicano intellectuals and artists. The word *Zeta* often appears in graffiti in East Los Angeles murals, alongside the ubiquitous *C/S*, meaning *con safos*, a collective signature of Chicano art. Not many Hispanic students know about him, but those who read him often find his writing electrifying, explosive. While estab-

lished historians of the Chicano movement, such as Rodolfo
Acuña and Carlos Muñóz, Jr., repeatedly ignore his work,
probably finding it unreliable, Zeta is a magnet for fiction
lovers: He appears, in cameos or as a protagonist, in a number of short stories and novels, and a Hollywood adaptation
of *The Revolt of the Cockroach People,* his second and last
published book, has been in the making for a decade. His
face is still a shadow next to César Chávez's or Rubén
Salazar's, the martyred Chicano journalist. In the making,
en estado larvario, that's how I would describe his present
status, in an ongoing stage of metamorphosis, slowly
approaching a pedestal. A Latin lover and *a fuckin' Mexican,* a freak, a rebel, a romantic husband, an idealist, a wan-
dering father, he was everywhere and nowhere at all times,
an identity in search of shape, a *yo* looking for *una
habitación propia,* a room of his own.

A CHUBBY PANZÓN

Annie Leibovitz was hired to take a photograph for the covers of Zeta's books, written in a "gonzo journalism" style—a technique, as Raymund A. Paredes puts it, "that requires the author's participation in the very events he is in the process of recording"—and detailing his strange and terrible pilgrimage from El Paso, Texas, to Oakland, California, from St. Louis to Las Vegas and East LA. He was originally from Modesto, California, some ninety-five miles and about an hour and a half southeast of San Francisco— *el nada modesto de Modesto*—but was raised in the San Joaquín Valley, and then, rambunctiously, lived on and off in California, Panama, Colorado, Mazatlán, Ciudad Juárez, Morelia, and elsewhere in the Southwest and south of the Rio Grande. His first volume, *The Autobiography of a Brown Buffalo,* appeared in 1972 under the imprint of Straight Arrow Books, a company attached to *Rolling Stone* magazine, for which Zeta's friend Hunter Thompson regularly wrote. Zeta personally considered it a masterpiece. How could he not? It was his lifelong achievement. He had spent every single day and night of his thirty-eight years drafting it, metaphorically and otherwise. Since early age he had been fond of writing his views of life and death, love and posterity. He had done so with passion but unsystematically, in an amateurish way, without ever perceiving himself as a professional novelist. Although he voraciously read Henry Miller and Jack Kerouac, he didn't admire them. He was fond of Miller's statement in *Tropic of Cancer*: "Every man with a bellyful of the classics is an enemy to the human race." And yet, his work reminds me of them both, especially the "automatic" approach to literature of the latter. In terms of style, his was free flowing, chaotic in structure and content, responding only to the goddess of spontaneity. He was absolutely clear about his tastes: "Ginsberg and those coffee houses with hungry-looking guitar players never did mean shit to me. *They* never took their drinking seriously. And the fact of the matter is that they got what was coming to them. It's their tough luck if they ran out and got on the road with bums like Kerouac, then came back a few years later with their hair longer and fucking marijuana up their asses, shouting Love and Peace and Pot. And still broke as ever."

He loved to manipulate data. An example among many. The end of his second book, *The Revolt of the Cockroach People,* takes place in 1972. In the last paragraph he announces he has just given up his career as a lawyer and plans to settle down to write. In a premonition, he argues he will soon meet a Tarascan princess in the Mexican state of Michoacán. He is of course referring to his second wife, Socorro, whom he first met in 1969 while she was a student at UCLA. The anachronism—by 1972 Zeta had already divorced her—serves him well: As a reference at the end of his narrative, the Tarascan beauty offers him a messianic, hopeful conclusion and a return *a las raíces,* to the sources. This lack of chronological coherence can become a biographer's ordeal. In his application for the California bar, for instance, Zeta's birthday is listed as April 8, 1935, but in *The Autobiography of a Brown Buffalo* he offers 1934 as the accurate birth year and some critics have used the date 1936. A lie? A mistake? Well, not really. Let's just call it a deceiving clue. Deception, after all, was Zeta's passion. The less others "categorized" him, *mejor.*

His father, Manuel Juan Acosta, ruled the house as a dictator. "I used to think that only my father was mad," he wrote once. Anita, aka Annie, one of Zeta's sisters, described the father-son relationship to me in an interview as quiet and respectful. "They definitely understood each other. Actually, he was very much in love with Dad. Very much." The father was a naturalized citizen who served in the U.S. Navy during World War II. Zeta sometimes called him The Captain in his writing. He was a janitor with a third-grade education. "My father was a little different than the other people where we lived," writes Zeta in an unpublished 1971 essay. "He wanted me to compete more than anything else so he pushed me into competition with himself. When I was five he encouraged me to argue and fight with him, which is unusual in a Mexican family. I guess that is where I became as nasty as I am." Elsewhere, he describes him as "an *indio* from the mountains of Durango. His father operated a mescal distillery before the revolutionaries drove him out. He met my mother while riding a motorcycle in El Paso." He adds: "[He] was a horse trader even though he got rid of both the mustache and the bike when FDR drafted him, a wetback, into the U.S. Navy on June 22, 1943. He tried to get into the marines, but when they found out he was a good swimmer and a noncitizen they put him in a sailor suit and made him drive a barge in Okinawa."

The word *indio* has a negative connotation. Exemplifying the divided collective self everywhere in Latin America, it is often used to offend someone, referring to him as uncivilized, uneducated, unmannered.[1] In Zeta's universe it was an ubiquitous term. In his autobiography, he writes: "My mother, for example, always referred to my father as *indio* when he'd get drunk and accuse her of being addicted to aspirin. If our neighbors got drunk at the baptismal parties and danced all night to *norteño* music, they were 'acting just like Indians.' Once I stuck my tongue in my sister Annie's mouth—I was practicing how to French kiss—and my ma wouldn't let me back in the house until I learned to 'quit behaving like an Indian.'"

Zeta's father wanted his son to give up *el español* and learn English in order to be *como los demás,* like everybody else. Zeta would resent this imposition for his entire life. In fact, his sense of rebelliousness, directly linked to the oppressive father image, became his signature. He was

[1]See my book *The Hispanic Condition: Reflections on Culture and Identity in America* (New York: HarperCollins, 1995), 109–10, 144–45.

careless and rambunctious, although he knew discipline was essential to shape an adolescent. Despite his claim to have been a *vato loco,* a wild street dude, after a distinguished career through high school he joined the air force in 1952, to prove he could live under a rigid disciplined environment. But his main interests were always beer and carousing.

A naturalized Texan from a working-class family, his mother, Juana Fierro Acosta, was a year younger than her husband. At one point in Zeta's autobiography he recalls the flour sacks she used to make dresses, shirts, and curtains. She loved music and could have been a singer, says Zeta, had she not married his father. He inherited her passion for music, becoming a clarinet player and always nurturing a love for jazz. He even got a music scholarship to the University of Southern California, but in the end decided not to pursue a career in music, probably for romantic reasons. As an adolescent, he would often play in bands. But he always disliked Mexican music, which, in his ears, was corny. His father was always working, and Zeta would often find himself wanting him back "because my mother was going crazy. She ate nothing but aspirins and oranges, drank black coffee and beat us with belts, rubber hoses, ice-hooks."

His upbringing was of course decisive in his *weltanshauung.* "Although I was born in El Paso, Texas," he once wrote, "I am actually a small town kid. A hick from the sticks, a Mexican boy from the other side of the tracks." Zeta would later on claim to be a descendant of Indians of Durango, a northern state in Mexico. "I grew up in River-

bank, California; post office box 303; population 3,969. It's
the only town in the entire state whose essential numbers
have remained unchanged. The sign that welcomes you as
you round the curve coming in from Modesto says, 'The
City of Action'." Riverbank, a rural community in the thir-
ties (Zeta used to pick peaches when he was a child), is
now part of Modesto, southwest of Oakdale and the Wood-
ward Reservoir. When his father was drafted in the U.S.
Navy during World War II, the child helped take care of
the household. He was intelligent and sensitive, coura-
geous and with bravado, but he suffered from a sense of
alienation, as if his place as a Chicano in society was ethe-
real, almost unreal, as if somebody was granting him permission to attend a party in which he could never feel
entirely comfortable. Zeta would eventually learn to love
and hate, *amar y odiar*, the Anglo establishment. Couldn't
live with the Anglos but couldn't live without them either.

The Acosta family owned two acres of land, in which
they planted corn, tomatoes, and yellow chiles. There were
a total of five children: three sisters and two brothers. Zeta
was the second son. The only things we have left of his
childhood, aside from the enlightening passages in his
autobiographical books, are a number of IDs, a handwritten exam he delivered for a history class, and a good grade
sheet for the 1949–1950 academic year at Oakdale Joint
Union High School. He got *C* and *C+* in English and
chemistry, but a uniform *A* in music and algebra. The
teacher reports that he keeps clean and neat, his desk is in
order, uses the English language well, is amiable, decent,
gracious, and a good sport. On the other hand, his teachers

frequently complained he didn't always obey orders promptly and at times failed to follow directions.

When I asked his sister Anita to recall a singular scene in Zeta's childhood encapsulating his future life, she invoked a mirror. "He would spend a long time in front of the mirror," she told me. "Grandiose, he felt grandiose from early on. He knew he had been called to play a historical role because when he was in front of the mirror, one got the feeling he was practicing. He was acting. Acting out the man he would later become." And indeed, his autobiography begins with a haunting image about obesity. "I stand naked before the mirror," writes Zeta.

Every morning of my life I have seen that brown belly from every angle. It has not changed that I can remember. I was always a fat kid. I suck it in and expand an enormous chest of two large hunks of brown tit. Possibly a loss of a pound here, a pound there? I put my hands to the hips, sandbaked elbows out like wings, and turn profiled to the floor-length reflection. I tighten, suck at the air and recall that Charles Atlas was a ninety-nine-pound weakling when the beach bully kicked sand in his girl friend's pretty face. Perhaps my old mother was right. I should lay off those Snicker bars, those liverwurst sandwiches with gobs of mayonnaise and those Goddamned caramel sundaes. But look, if I suck it in just a wee bit more, push that bellybutton up against the back; can you see what will surely come to pass if you but rid yourself of this extra flesh? Just think of all the broads you'll get if you trim down to a comfortable 200.

The repercussions of the move by the Acosta family to Riverbank would later on appear in one of his unpublished short stories, "The Little House." Although he excelled as a student and in sports, was president of his high school class, and a Boy Scout in Troop 42, he began to abuse alcohol at Oakdale Joint Union High School, and at age eighteen experienced his first ulcers. Indeed, his rebellious spirit and anti-Americanism can be tracked down to a very important scene in Zeta's autobiography when, as a child between eight and ten years of age, he spits on the American flag. He and a number of Mexican boys were marching single file in front of the old PT&T in his hometown, when he saw a leaflet with the picture of the American flag and spit.

> "Hey, look what Oscar did," Johnny Gomez tells the others. He stands back, points to the leaflet as if it were some snake. The others circle around and shake their heads.
> "What'd you do that for?" his brother, David, demands of me.
> "Why not? It's just a picture," I explain.
> "That's the American flag, stupid!"
> "So what?"
> "So don't do it no more."
> "Why? You gonna make me?"

Zeta refuses to apologize, and the kids start a fight. He fights "each of them that afternoon. I lost every single fight." Again, the experience would leave a deep scar. Like

Cervantes's protagonist Alonso Quijano, he would spend his life fighting gigantic windmills, struggling against invisible ghosts. Life would be perceived as an ongoing war against astute evil forces always difficult to pinpoint. Not until his adulthood, when Zeta recognized racism and injustice as his primary enemies, would he understand what his battles were against.

One of Zeta's anxieties had to do with his small penis. His rampant machismo could not hide his sense of confusion and lack of self-esteem, directly linked to his minuscule *pajarito*. He feared becoming *un marica,* a homosexual, and spent his adolescence competing against his fellowmen, proving himself, showing off. And he spent his life thinking his penis was too insignificant, which, in his words, automatically turned him into a fag. "Frugality and competition were [our] lot," he writes when describing his and his brother's education. "The truth of it was [my parents] conspired to make men out of two innocent Mexican boys. It seems that the sole purpose of childhood was to train boys how to be men. Not men of the future, but *now.* We had to get up early, run home from school, work on weekends, holidays and during vacations, all for the purpose of being men. We were supposed to talk like *un hombre,* walk like a man, act like a man and think like a man." His whole oeuvre is invested with remarks about his psychological complex: the small size of his phallus. He recurrently perceived himself as a freak, a virile metastasis. "If it hadn't been for my fatness," he argues, "I'd probably have been able to do those fancy assed jackknifes and swan dives as well as the rest of you. But [when] my mother had me conceived I was obese, ugly as a pig and without any redeeming qualities whatsoever. How then could I run around with just my jockey shorts? V-8s don't hide fat, you know. That's why I finally started wearing boxers. But by then it was too late. Everyone knew I had the smallest prick in the world. With the girls watching and giggling, the guys used to sing my private song to the tune of 'Little Bo Peep': 'Oh, where, oh where can my little boy be? Oh, where, oh where can he be? He's so chubby, *panzón,* that he can't move along. Oh, where, oh where can he be?' "

Zeta felt impotent and wandered around questioning his earthly stature. He constantly identified with tough guys like Charles Atlas, James Cagney, Edward G. Robinson, and Humphrey Bogart, but ended up frustrated. "I lost most of my religion the same night I learned about sex from old Vernon," he claims.

When I saw the white, foamy suds come from under his foreskin, I thought he had wounded himself from yanking on it too hard with those huge farmer hands of his. And when I saw his green eyes fall back into his head, I thought he was having some sort of seizure like I'd seen Toto the village idiot have out in his father's orchard after he fucked a chicken. I didn't much like the sounds of romance the first time I saw jizz. I knew that Vernon was as tough as they came. Nothing frightened or threatened him. He'd cuss right in front of John Hazard, our fag Boy Scout leader as well as Miss Anderson. But when I heard him OOOh and AAAh as the soap suds spit at his chest while we lay on our backs inside the pup tent, I wondered

for a minute if sex wasn't actually for sissies. I tried to follow his example, but nothing would come out. With him
cheering me on, saying "Harder, man. Pull on that son of
a bitch. Faster, faster!" it just made matters worse. The
thing went limp before the soap suds came out. . . . He
advised me to try it more often. "Don't worry, man. It'll
grow if you work on it."

As expected in a Catholic family like the Acostas, religious love played a fundamental role in his early life. While
his folks were not openly religious, he started attending the
Catholic Church in his youth. Somebody stationed at
Hamilton Air Force Base, near San Francisco, started
telling him stories about Baptists. "Everybody at the
church saw me as being really different," he wrote in 1971.
"I was a Chicano, a musician, a Catholic and a sinner. So all
of the little chicks dug me and loved to hear me tell about
all of my sins. This blew my mind and I started going to
the church. Within a few months, I was converted. I saw
Jesus coming down from a cloud one night. I got saved,
really, Billy Graham style. Being the fanatic I am I became
a preacher immediately. . . ." He employed his days and
nights voraciously reading the Bible, which had an incredi-
ble effect. He meditated on the "malevolent" impact of
Christianity in the region and felt ashamed of sharing the
faith in Christ and the Church. Soon after, he converted
and became a Baptist, and religion took over his entire life.

JESUS AND
A CAT'S MEOW

Zeta often liked to describe his existential journey as divided into three major traumas. The first had to do with his first love affair. He fell for a white-skinned, Anglo-Saxon girl who he calls Jane Addison in his first book. He describes his infatuation in some detail in *The Autobiography of a Brown Buffalo*. Her parents rejected him because of his ethnic background and skin color. They had met in fourth grade, and their relationship grew very strong. At one point they even contemplated marriage. But the difficulties were overwhelming, and Zeta decided to disappear by joining the air force. He just couldn't handle it. The scar of the racial division between lovers would haunt him forever. Jane was an archetype: an intelligent blonde personifying the whole mainstream establishment. She was a Dulcinea to Zeta's Don Quixote. He was ready to sort out any obstacle to prove his devotion. But the barriers were too strong to be dismantled: at one point, Jane herself humiliates him by telling a teacher that Zeta stank, implying that all *mexicanos* expel a distinctively unpleasant body odor. *¡Prohibida la entrada a perros y a mexicanos!* He was outraged and couldn't stand it.

Zeta and Jane's Shakespearean liaison, à la Romeo and Juliet, cannot fail to remind us of the Broadway musical *West Side Story,* that bottomless pit through whose pathos mainstream America stereotypes Hispanic youth. Acosta is Tony and Jane Addison is María, although in reverse. Racially different, he is rejected by an Anglo family in which whiteness translates as purity and redemption. Brown—the color of the buffalo—is beginning to stick in Zeta's mind. He knows he's *prieto.* No matter how much success he achieves in high school, he will always be part of *la raza de bronce.* His skin color would determine his isolation in Anglo-Saxon America. Although Tony dies in the musical, Acosta will take a different path. He will be forced to go through life existentially injured, his self scarred. Ethnic exclusion will ignite in him dreams of destruction.

His second adolescent love was a young lady he addresses as June MacAdoo, a revision, a new version of Jane Addison provoking an essentially different affair. Zeta had a serious crush on her, which broke up prior to his departure for Oakland and his long journey in search of himself. June, it seems, hesitated to make a full commitment to him, one, in Zeta's terms, because he kept procrastinating about a wedding date, and as is evident in his letters, she eventually had another sweetheart she was ready to marry. Occasionally the names Jane and June pop up in his books, always denoting a problematic sentimental past. But Zeta's most complex, ultimately disturbing romance

was with Alice Joy, a high school classmate. "Alice could
cry better than any woman I've known in my life," he
claimed. He called her Miss It, the perfect woman. The
sister of a friend, Alice was a thirteen-year-old farmer's
daughter from Riverbank. As Zeta discusses in his autobiography, her father had been an alcoholic whom her
mother divorced, only to marry a deacon from Arkansas
who tried to rape Alice at age twelve. Add to it the fact that
the man wholeheartedly hated Mexicans.

"She's the cat's meow," Tim Watkins, one of Zeta's
acquaintances, told him at the time. "I'm telling you. Cans
up to her chin and an ass like a brick shithouse. I've never
seen a better looking snatch in my whole life." It was 1951
when Zeta saw her and he immediately knew she was *el
amor de su vida*. It was instant passion. Alice also knew
one of Zeta's sisters and was thus familiar with him. He
courted her. He wanted to make her his property. But his
knight attitude didn't take him very far. As in the case of
Jane Addison, the issue of skin color quickly emerged, seasoned with religious connotations. His autobiography
devotes more than fifteen pages to describe their affair.
She was from a Baptist background, and the fact that the
Acostas were Catholic became an insurmountable barrier.
"Daddy says some Catholics don't believe in Jesus," Alice
told Zeta, to which he replied: "You can tell him this one
does. He's my favorite saint."

Youthful love is often overwhelmed by a dose of pathological obsession one learns to overcome with age. Zeta
needed to be close to Alice. He wanted to breath through
her nostrils, see through her eyes, palpitate inside her skin.

She, in turn, was attracted to him, although she saw his need for sexual discovery as an adventure way beyond her religion's boundaries—way beyond what she was ready to challenge. "It wasn't a matter of my beastly sex life," he would later on write. "It was my family name. When she told her mother the name of her new boyfriend, the old bag said no dice. Never. Forget it. And she was never to speak to me again. In fact, she made her write [a] letter so that she wouldn't have to explain the situation to me in person." The couple were deeply attached, and although her parents never liked him, he didn't stop at anything. Zeta nominated Alice for a beauty pageant called Oracle Queen. He was her manager and publicity agent. She ended up winning, and he was, quite literally, *full of Joy*. But the Acostas and the Joys finally got the police to separate them. Zeta was angry and lost his temper. *"¡Chinga tu madre, cabrón!"* he began shouting. Nothing could be done. A few months later Alice sent him a letter telling him she had married a dark-skinned Italian Catholic, the guy who told Zeta he'd love to eat Alice's snatch.

Alice Joy brought Zeta to his third trauma: religion. The knowledge of the Baptist faith he got from her was enough to make him switch faiths. He had not been able to get the girl, but he didn't want to run away from her milieu. So he mastered the Baptist gospel. The attitude highlights Zeta's response to catastrophe. A bit like the impostor protagonist at the heart of Woody Allen's film *Zelig*, rather than escaping his enemies, Zeta devoted his energy to understanding their mentality and, furthermore, becoming one of them. If Mohammed cannot reach the mountain, let the mountain reach Mohammed. He gave up Catholicism and was elected president of the Young People's Club of the Petaluma Baptist Church, in town, "because I could testify to more sin and corruption than these egg farmers had ever dreamed existed." He soon converted his whole family to the Baptist religion, with the sole exception of his brother, Robert.

A bit earlier he had decided to become a professional musician and spent long hours playing the clarinet. Then, immediately after high school, Zeta enlisted in the air force, from where he would be honorably discharged in 1956, after four years of service. Before that, he was shipped to Panama in 1952, where he stayed for a couple of years and helped set up about five missions. Down there he became a Baptist minister in a leper colony and proselytized among local people. He built a mission in a place named Chilibre, "a small village with black Jamaicans and brown Panamanians," and became known as the Mexican Billy Graham. He would go around telling people, "You need God! Find Him! He will save your soul!" But once again, troublesome questions, this time about faith, began to emerge. "When I had about six months left to go [in Panama] I realized I was going crazy so I made a last, final study to see if what I was teaching was true," he wrote. "I made a study of the gospels and, on one side of the page I put the things I felt good about, and, on the other, the things I felt bad about, in comparing the life of Jesus. Within three months that bad side was about twenty times heavier than the good side so I no longer believed in him. That caused the second big trauma in my life. Here I didn't believe in him and I had a hundred people believing in me in my congregations. I had Indians, Panamanians, servicemen of all races. They looked at me as their pastor. So for three months I had to go on preaching and teaching shit that I didn't believe. That really affected my whole thing with the result that when I got out of the service I attempted suicide. Naturally I chickened out like everybody else but I ended up in psychiatry."

This persona, Zeta as Baptist minister, and the three *amigas*—Jane, June, and Alice—acquired a peculiar mental dimension in his psyche. He saw these experiences as failed masculine challenges, *la pérdida de la masculinidad,* and from then on unconsciously assumed the personality of a disoriented macho. Rather than stimulating a less violent, more sensitive response, his milieu immediately accepted his phalocentric ways. Machismo prevailed in the Hispanic world north of the Rio Grande. Its idiosyncratic reveries date back to 1523, when Hernán Cortés subdued the Aztec city of Tenochtitlán, known today as Mexico City. Courage and the obsessive art of glorifying the phallus were the norm in the New World, and the *braceros* and wetbacks crossing the border carried along the tradition.

Zeta is an example of genetic continuity. Spanish Catholicism instituted in the Americas the concept of original sin, and in colonial times, it generated a sense of shame and dislike for women. Nudity was forbidden in public spaces but abused in privacy. The Iberian knights who crossed the Atlantic, unlike their Puritan counterparts in the British Colonies, were fortune-driven bachelors. They did not come to settle down, to find a new Promised

Land. As Cortés wrote to Charles V in his *Cartas de Relación*, the first conquistadors were pure trash: rough, primitive, and uneducated people from lowly origins. Their goal was to expand the territorial and symbolic powers of the Spanish crown. They were in the new continent to find gold and pleasure. And pleasure they found in the bare-breasted Indian women, whom they raped at will and then abandoned. Eroticism was a fundamental element in the colonization of the Hispanic world. It was ubiquitous from Cuzco to Chichén Itzá and Uxmal. Evidently the pre-Columbian population did not outlaw sex, but the clash with the Spaniards generated a magisterial, still-unhealed rape scene. The Latin phallus, not gunpowder, was the ultimate weapon used to subdue.

Another important player, the Church's hypocritical attitude, cannot be minimized. In Latin America most priests (notable exceptions are Fray Bartolomé de Las Casas and Fray Toribio de Benavente, aka Motolinía) stood witness to the abrasive, strident sexuality of Spanish soldiers. *Fingieron demencia*: they closed their eyes, they pretended to be elsewhere. Simultaneously, they reproduced the medieval hierarchy of sexes that prevailed in Europe: man as king, woman as servant and reproductive machine. In his insightful book *Demons in the Convent*, the journalist and anthropologist Fernando Benítez eloquently described the fashion in which, in the seventeenth century, the Church established an atmosphere of repressed eroticism. The archbishop of Mexico City, Aguiar y Seijas, who walked with crutches and nourished a thousand phobias (among them, a hatred for water), detested women to the point of not allowing them to be in his presence. If in a convent or monastery a nun walked in front of him, he would ipso facto cover his eyes. Only men were worthy of his sight—men and Christ. Not surprisingly, in the continent's religious paraphernalia Jesus and the many almighty saints appear almost totally unclothed, covering only their private parts with what in Spanish is known as *taparrabo*, loincloths, whereas the Virgen de Guadalupe, the Virgen de la Caridad, the Virgen del Cobre, and a thousand other virgins in the Caribbean, Mexico, and South America, are fully dressed. Might their flesh be dangerous and lascivious? Impure and satanic?[1] Zeta's hyperactive, incredibly convoluted machismo fits well the cultural habitat he came from. He is a modern Hernán Cortés, a *conquistador* always looking for women to subjugate, to possess and oppress. Is he therefore less guilty? Obviously not. His machismo was a source of strength and also a form of shame and embarrassment. He was envious, covetous, jealous. As a Baptist priest, he preached restraint, but deep inside, his natural instinct possessed him. He saw women as sheer objects of pleasure. He rejoiced in their nudity and eroticism in private but found it disgraceful in public. Women were either *vírgenes* or *putas*, virgins or whores. When married, he was unfaithful to his wife but asked her for chastity and forbid her promiscuity. Betty Daves, to whom Zeta wrote emotionally charged letters until 1971, told me: "He often had violent outbursts. He would per-

[1] See my essay "The Latin Phallus," *Transition* 65 (Spring 1995), 48–68.

ceive all women as potential lovers. Never equal partners. Jane and June and Alice. . . . They left a scar in him. He never overcame the emotional drainage he suffered when he loved them. You have to remember that the Acosta family stimulated that type of male behavior. At one point, Oscar's brother, Bob, made an advance to me. He wanted for us to go to bed together."

In spite of his unquestionable ambiguity toward the opposite sex, while Zeta was married to Betty Daves Dowd (1956–1963) he found in her guidance and security. The couple changed addresses several times within the state of California and also lived briefly with Betty's parents, in Maplewood and St. Louis, Missouri. They lived together on and off, often separating because of Zeta's jealousy rides or violent reactions. "I feel the need to again apologize for my behavior," he wrote in a letter. "I know I've not acted with reason for the past month. The reason for this eccentric behavior is at this time unimportant. All I know is that I have, and more important is the frustrating realization that I cannot of my own volition deter from this course without tremendous amount of inhibition and repression." Elsewhere, he claimed: "It's a funny thing, honey, what I've learned about you and marriage since we've been separated this time. I have realized what you used to mean when you told me that a man had to put his family before others. I never consciously placed others above you or my responsibilities to you or Marco, but I guess in many ways I was." Sometime later, he added: "*Ma chérie*, I don't want to write because I'm feeling bad, but yet I feel compelled since there is only myself to talk to. . . . I'll be fine, eventually (what a damn long nebulous word). You say you feel 'At peace.' How I envy you. I don't. I'm confused. Where in the hell am I? I feel that I need help, but I don't believe in it, so what shall I do? Do as I feel or as I believe? The latter will be the one I'll take even though it is harder. I don't believe in paying some other man to help me. . . ." Zeta could be affectionate and endearing in his correspondence, if also a bit childish at times. "Marco's toilet brings me laughs each time I walk into the bedroom. I want to take a picture of him sitting on it before long. We've just got to start taking more pictures or else we'll be sorry in our old age. Memories are the best source of comfort for those past the age of discovery, which we will be some day whether we like it or not, so we'd better get some system worked up soon." His archives at UCSB are full of Western Union telegrams in which he sends Betty his love and, simultaneously, asks for money to be wired to him. He dreamed of having a normal family life: his own apartment, a steady job, nice furniture, weekend time to enjoy with his wife and son. But the recurrent response to his wishful thinking was more emotional turmoil, more instability. Consequently, the overall impression one gets while reading his letters to Betty is that of a besieged couple, she trying desperately to keep him away from trouble in order to save their souls, he doing as much as he could to make sense of his increasing insanity.

DR. SERBIN'S
HONORABLE MENTION

Zeta met Betty at a Modesto hospital, where she was an occupational therapist. Their relationship, let me stress it again, was nothing but bumpy. Like Jane, June, and Alice, Betty was a WASP whose father, although cordial, often displayed racist feelings against Mexicans. Zeta would hide his drug addiction from her and would frequently feel jealous after any accidental response she had to another man. Their son, Marco Federico Manuel Acosta, was born in 1959, when Zeta was twenty-five, shortly after he was hospitalized in Sausalito, after a street fight with some Germans. "He was extremely antagonistic," claims Betty. Supporting a family of three wasn't at all easy. He was ferocious with his employers, vociferous with friends and family members, often physically violent. He would get drunk and would not come back at night. Consequently, he was repeatedly fired, and holding a single job proved extremely hard. At the same time, he was a consummate actor. He would eventually find a way to persuade people to hire him back or help him out with money. "He could sell you any piece of garbage he wanted, that's how convincing he was," argues Betty. "Once he convinced a chemical company to give him a job as a junior chemist. It was simply unbelievable!" His bad behavior would sooner or later backfire. He would feel remorse, sorrow, and anguish. In postcards and correspondence, he would apologize. "Betty, please write to me," he asks. "And once again, please send me a picture of you and Marco. Go to a studio and have a good one made. Bye for now, my lovely wife." And elsewhere: "I haven't gotten a job yet," Zeta wrote from San Francisco. "Things are very slow around here. Unemployment is at a high peak all over the state. I have several leads, though. Tuesday I'm going to the Foster cafeteria joint. They say that they are always hiring. I have a couple of other places in mind." He continues: "I saw the doctor yesterday and he said that he thought it was very important for me to get a job . . . not just for financial reasons either."

His obesity, his ulcers, and a failing heart (according to Marco Acosta, Zeta suffered a stroke in the fifties) made him physically vulnerable and the day-to-day insanity would color his behavior as a husband and father. Both his parents and Betty encouraged him to seek therapeutic help, but it took him a while to accept their plea. He entered psychiatric treatment in the fall of 1957 and spent a total of ten years under the supervision of Dr. William Serbin, a Jewish doctor. They met when Serbin was an intern at Mount Zion Hospital, near Divisadero. "A girl from St. Louis suggested I visit Mt. Zion to see if they might have a cure for my ulcers," Zeta would write in

1972. "The first time I applied they told me I wasn't sick enough to get on their emergency list and instead gave me a list of names of various private psychiatrists in San Francisco." He had three sessions with one Dr. Rubinstein, at twenty-five dollars an hour. He was then referred to Dr. Serbin, who was still in practice in San Francisco at the time of my research but repeatedly refused to answer my phone calls. As he put it, I "spent the entire time arguing about the cost of the service." When his first book begins, in 1967, Zeta is ready to quit his job and finish his psychiatric treatment with Dr. Serbin once and for all. He is sure it has not helped him a bit. He is tired of psychoanalysis and thinks of Freud as a consummate fool. "After ten years I turn my back on that Jew with his ancient history hang ups," he writes. Elsewhere, he says: "In ten years of therapy the only thing the fucker has wanted to gossip about has been my mother and my ancestry. 'Sex and race. It's one and the same hang up.' He doesn't seem to understand that my ulcers didn't arrive until I was around eighteen. But he is hung up on ancient history. Moses and Freud really got him."

Dr. Serbin is portrayed as a figure that haunts him. While he fires him "for incompetence" early on in the narrative, he will reappear in flashbacks, as a Goya monster, an ubiquitous ghost. Obviously Zeta was Dr. Serbin's Portnoy of sort: a neurotic patient with unresolved ties to his mother and father, the embodiment of excess, a drunk, a perverse sexual dreamer, a pathological liar, and an impossible complainer. When I imagine their therapeutic sessions, I see an overwhelmed Zeta in the process of explain-

ing his mental maze while an inexperienced psychiatrist
tries out alternative solutions that invariably lead nowhere.
Against all odds, Dr. Serbin kept on fighting. *"Por diosito!"*
Zeta would tell him repeatedly. "Just think, you'll get hon-
orable mention in the numerous books they'll write about
me when I'm famous." Zeta's mental instability was difficult to diagnose. He would oscillate between periods of
sheer creative madness and schizophrenic outburst,
between manic depression and destructive fury. Perhaps
more than anything else, Zeta was a relentless paranoid. In
this regard Dr. Serbin's Judaism is quite relevant. Time and
again, Zeta would perceive his therapist as a greedy profi-
teer, a rapacious, gluttonous doctor using Freud's theory to
empty a Chicano's wallet. Indeed, their liaison serves as a
magnifying glass of Zeta's views of Jews and other ethnic
groups. Although in his writing and as an activist he doesn't
quite come across as an anti-Semite, he often portrayed
Mexican-Americans as a misunderstood and mistreated
minority regularly exploited by others higher in the social
hierarchy. He also thought others were out to get him—an
orchestrated plot by his enemies was always about to cru-
cify him.

In 1956, after he was discharged from the air force and
before he met Dr. Serbin, he tried to commit suicide in
New Orleans. Although we lack irrefutable documenta-
tion, he most probably repeated the attempt once or twice
more throughout the next decade and a half. Life seemed
an intricate labyrinth. He doubted his potential for control.
He had been rejected by women in his hometown, and the
entire experience as a preacher in Panama was incredibly

shocking. Was there a point in continuing? What was expected from him? Would he ever make a difference? Would he find the *voz interna*, the inner call that could direct his behavior? At first he returned to Riverbank to live at his parents' home. He spent his time having sex and living a hedonistic life. He also attended Modesto Junior College and then went to San Francisco State University, where he devoted most of his time to creative writing. After his loss of Christian faith and his "Mexican Billy Graham" identity in Central America, he concluded that if ever he was going to achieve anything *en la vida,* he needed discipline and responsibility, *disciplina y responsabilidad,* two values both his father and the army had overstressed. Discipline and responsibility. He began working as a copy boy at the *San Francisco Examiner.* His grade point average in college doesn't have the level of excellence he had shown in high school. He was distracted, his attention placed in sexual adventures, music, and whatnot. Nothing above standard in his youthful performance. He worked as a dishwasher and performed other menial jobs. He traveled to Vail, Colorado. He wasn't sure what he wanted to be. *¿Músico? ¿Matemático?* In high school he excelled in exact sciences and wondered whether graduate school in the field was a convenient option. But his artistic sensibility also played a fundamental role in his day-to-day endeavors. Should he instead follow a more Bohemian calling?

He suffered more nervous breakdowns. One occurred in October 1959, soon after Marco was born. Apparently Zeta's identity as a father went wild. He had been smoking

pot and meddled with dangerous drugs. He couldn't come
to terms with the new responsibilities, with the new weight
on his shoulders. One early morning, Betty found him
totally frozen. "He was sitting outside, paralyzed," she told
me. "What could I do? My mother worked in St. Luke's.
We went to a drugstore to buy some medicine. Sheer madness. . . . He wouldn't respond. He obviously was frustrated, depressed, disappointed with himself. Now that he
was turning into *un padre*, he couldn't feel a sense of self-
fulfillment. Since early on he had nourished titanic
dreams: to write the Great American Novel, to become the
Great American Lawyer, to be known and applauded." But
the birth of his son made him feel belittled—a cockroach.
His response: he took to the road and made himself lost.
Ciao, adiós, arrivederci, and bye bye. Vanished, suddenly
and without explanation. *Desapareció, como por arte de
magia.* Such disappearances were frequent during his marriage to Betty. Through postcards and letters filled with
emotional power, he would tell his wife and baby son about
his search for his identity. "I'll be back . . . Luv'ya." In
truth, he was incapable of handling his own affairs.

The getaway led to nowhere and Zeta was hospitalized
at San Francisco County General Hospital, in Potrero
Hill. Whenever his state of mind improved, he would be
allowed to work in a training camp. He was under a treatment of amphetamines and needed to clean up his system. We have a letter by Dr. Serbin himself in his files at
UCSB, addressed to Zeta's wife, Betty, dated May 13,
1960, shortly after Marco was born in 1959, and written
on stationery of the Department of Psychiatry of Mount

Zion Hospital and Medical Center in San Francisco. It reads:

Dear Mrs. Acosta:

Although we have never met, I have felt you would want to know my opinion of your husband's present status. The last several months have been extremely stable and comfortable ones for him. He has been able to renounce a previous abundance of self—and eventually self-destructive—needs in favor of the more difficult and rewarding goals of regular work, self-respect and emotional maturity. His tolerance of frustration and disappointment has markedly increased; more important, he is involved in being of service to others, in his work at Juvenile Work. I feel these changes are crucial ones and would be most helpful of his continuing success. If I can be of further help, please let me know.

Very truly yours,

William M. Serbin, M.D.

In Zeta's black-and-white universe, doctors were victimizers, cruel, unmerciful oppressors. When he finally got out of the San Francisco hospital, his antagonism toward the medical establishment did not cease. Years later, on September 1965, for example, he wrote a letter to the doctor's hospital in Modesto, where, as he puts it, he was given improper care. A few months before, in May, at 11 P.M., he had been rushed to the emergency room in a deplorable mental state, but bureaucratic obstacles stopped him from being seen by a doctor. The staff, as he wrote it, demanded

some $300 in cash and refused to honor his insurance
company, Kaiser. The interns coerced his father, who was
accompanying him, to sign a document saying that Zeta
alone was responsible for his action. He was forced to stay
overnight and, in his view, was pushed to a terrible psychological situation. He called the whole incident "humiliating."
"Notice is hereby given of denial of any and all alleged
obligations whether express or implied purportedly made
by myself, Oscar Acosta, or by any agent or representative,
including Manuel Acosta and Juana F. Acosta." He added:
You "knowingly and wilfully confined me in the boundaries
of your hospital premises against my will with the specific
intent to deprive me of the freedom of bodily movement
which I made known to you and your agents and represen-
tatives; such demand is made for compensation in the sum
of $500.00 for the injury suffered. . . ."

His psychiatric intractability had enormous ramifica-
tions. The moment he left Dr. Serbin, Zeta became a heavier drug abuser. He learned to live with his ulcers and
mental unbalances and, moreover, to believe in dreams
and hallucinations. In the early seventies, however, he
seemed to have struck a fragile, secure balance. He trusted
his messianic powers and devoted his energy to the pursuit
of his politics. In the unpublished 1971 essay, he wrote that

> one thing I haven't mentioned enough yet [in my work],
> which is a very pertinent thing, is what drugs have done
> for me personally. I think psychedelic drugs have been
> important to the development of my consciousness. I
> don't think I'd have gotten to where I am without the use

of these drugs. They've put me into a level of awareness where I can see myself and see what I'm really doing. Most of the big ideas I've gotten for my lawyer work have usually come when I am stoned. Like the Grand Jury challenge was the result of an acid experience. A lot of the tactics I employ I get the ideas for when I am stoned, which is not to say that I wouldn't get them if I wasn't stoned. A lot of my creativity has sprung from the use of these psychedelic drugs.

He was of course part of an era that idolized the shaman as an anti-establishment figure of profound knowledge, a period in history in which alternative approaches to body and mind, from mushrooms to herbal drugs, theoreticians from Felix Guattari to David Cooper, were in vogue. Zeta was interested in marginal states of consciousness and psychedelic trips as *unio mystica,* as a link to his proto-Mexican self. By acknowledging that society, not himself, was sick, he ultimately became his own healer. He at once internalized and subverted Dr. Serbin's technique: Zeta as self-therapist.

DEAR MISS SHRIFTE

Suddenly writing took center stage. The Zeta of the late
fifties, Betty's husband and Marco's father, comes across as
a literary apprentice in search of a voice. He wrote everything he saw, everything he thought. *Escribo, luego existo.*
He seemed to be looking for a theme to put his hands on,
un libro, a book to write. Those that knew him at the time
remember him as scribbling frantically. He needed listen-
ers, needed to see his work published and thus began to
send his manuscript to editors as early as 1962. "They were
wonderful tales," Betty remembered. "Oscar was an extraordinary writer, full of passion, impatient. . . . But he never
found a way to sell his stuff. In his correspondence he
always notified me of rejects. 'It doesn't matter,' he would
say. 'One day they'll beg for it!' He just wasn't a business-
man when it came to selling his work." Around that time
Zeta showed his early stories to friends, some of whom he
had met at San Francisco State College and the *Examiner,*
like Douglas Empringham and Mark Harris. Harris, for
one, recommended what others had already told him:

"You've got to make up your mind what you want to be. . . .
Is it going to be math? Or are you going to be a writer?"
Harris's own advice was that he drop out of school and pursue a literary career, no matter what the outcome. According to Betty, he would write everywhere and at all hours—
at home and away, in the morning and after dinner, on
napkins and toilet paper. A number of literary projects
seemed to be cooking (short stories, a play, a long narrative), but none materialized. At least not immediately.

Literature offered Zeta a therapeutic cure unavailable
anywhere else. In a letter to his wife, he says: "I've been
working quite a bit on the book. I wish I had a reader. . . ."
He was most probably referring to a finished first novel,
My Cart for My Casket, which he sent to various publishers without success. In a January 1963 letter, he writes:

Dear Miss Shrifte,

I am sending you this m.s. unsolicited because in *The
Writer's Handbook,* 1960 edition, it states that you are interested in books of a 'provocative nature.' Two years ago, when
I finished this, my first novel, I thought it was provocative.
Now I cannot bear the sight of it. I would be willing to sell it
for publication for the cost of mailing, which after five publishers is approximately ten (10) dollars. I have continued to
write and I hope to mature in my writing since *My Cart.* I
am presently working on another novel which I believe is
much superior to this one and I hope truly provocative; it,
like this one, deals with the Mexicans and the Oakies in the
San Joaquín Valley, but deals more with the question, Is the
answer to the problem Religion or Politics? Etcetera. I wish I

knew how to talk or write about my writing. But it is too
close to me. If you see any "promise" or "ability," . . . let me
know if you are interested, since as the *Handbook* said, this is
what you are looking for in new writers.

Zeta's fruitful career as a reader came to a stop. He
ceased to read fiction in the late fifties because, as he wrote,
it was "a waste of times." His passions had been for Dylan
Thomas and Konrad Lorenz. But he couldn't concentrate.
Besides, he wanted to be read, not to read. He wrote a considerable amount of bad poetry. As far as I've been able to
track them down, none of his poems were ever published.
They are part of his archives at UCSB and help map his
existential journey. Many don't amount to more than sheer
mumbling. In that respect, they resemble the poetic
endeavors of another early Hispanic writer in the United
States, Felipe Alfau (b. 1902), the author of two groundbreaking novels, *Locos: A Comedy of Gestures* and *Chro-
mos: A Parody.* Sometime between 1929 and the sixties,
Alfau wrote many romantic poems in Spanish.[1] They serve
as a compass when attempting to understand the writer's
creative and linguistic odyssey. Likewise with Zeta. Here, for
instance, is an untitled poem by Zeta dated November 1967.

> How many echoes of the sublime
> would inform us of reality's line.
> To see the shape take all the

[1] I translated and introduced them in 1992 in the volume *Sentimental Songs* (Naperville, Ill.: Dalkey Archive Press, 1992).

poets' lines and super-impose upon
the words of the Christ.

Hear is here—

The one surfaced two surfaced living
symbol
wartime, love time, wait time—
a present from time in
form of Present time
pictures saved from eons
reprojected ions—for
pleasure—for pain—
for meaning—for
change
small change—social change
and do you know anyone
who makes a loaf of good bread?

Nothing memorable. Or take the following one, written
in March 1966, part of an ongoing series entitled "Poems
for Spring Days":

Some guys think Baldwin's got it bad.
Hell no one ever knows me, let alone my name.
I can cry loud as hell
You think that'll bring 'em out?

Have you ever counted the days I've sat here
Waiting for you to come and feed me,

Or have you ever stopped to think
How many times I've cried
For Moctezuma's dead son?
Hell no, you've never ever learned
To count,
let alone my miseries.

Angry is as angry does.
Cute, no?

If it's true
dead men tell no tales
then let's kill 'em all
to stop their wails.

A missy named Gail
Was kept in the jail
For raising her dress
Instead of her bail.

Simultaneously, Zeta wrote a number of short stories of
various quality, hoping to place them either as a collection
or interrelating them and thus approaching the volumes as
a novel. Rumors have it that *My Cart for My Casket* was
originally called *Perla Is a Pig*, which was the title of one of
its earlier chapters. I was told by Betty and Marco that the
manuscript is perhaps stored somewhere in the late
Socorro Aguiniga's attic. They share the impression of having seen the book. At any rate, its shape and structure
remain a mystery. Since it presumably was a finished prod-

uct, something his stories at the UCSB archives are not, finding it would help us understand Zeta's early literary endeavors.

As an autonomous text, "Perla Is a Pig" was Zeta's only published piece of short fiction and has great value in tracking his existential odyssey. It originally appeared in the short-lived Chicano magazine *Con Safos* in 1970, a forum in which ethnic, ideological, and cultural matters, particularly Chicano affairs, were put forward, and was later collected in the anthology *Voices of Aztlán*.[2] Long before its final appearance, Zeta sent it to a handful of New York publishers, from Alfred A. Knopf to Macmillan, apparently not realizing it was too short for publication in book form. "Of course you realize that this is nothing that we would publish either by itself or in combination of other short stories of yours. Books of short stories are simply not marketable objects in present-day hard book publishing," wrote Macmillan's executive editor, Cecil Scott, in 1962. And then came the usual, if disappointing words of encouragement: "Whenever you find yourself committed to a full-length book, be quite sure that I shall be most happy to read the manuscript when it is ready."

Divided into three parts, with a total of about 7,500 words, the text shows Zeta at his most lyrical and straightforward. It evidences an influence of writers like John Steinbeck, Erskine Caldwell, and Ernest Hemingway, and probably also of south-of-the-border masters like Agustín

[2]*Voices of Aztlán: Chicano Literature Today,* edited by Dorothy E. Harth and Lewis M. Baldwin (New York: Mentor, 1974), 28–48.

Yáñez and Juan Rulfo, although it's unclear to me if Zeta was ever acquainted with their work in Spanish. Set in a Mexican barrio, the plot centers on the troubled friendship of an old man, known as *el huero*, "the blond one," the owner of a fat, corn-eating pig, and his business partner, Nicolás Bordona, aka Nico. Because of his light-colored skin, *el huero* is known as a gringo in the neighborhood. This distinguishes him from the rest and often makes him a target of animosity. All sorts of rumors circulate about his depraved self: one suggests he pees on the field to make his corn grow; another, that he suffers from leprosy. People avoid him, and Nico, abusive and egotistic, is always trying to find ways to make him more appealing, less abstruse. Among his strategies is the selling of the pig as butcher's meat, to earn money. But as it turns out, no matter what he does, *el huero* will always be marginalized.

Zeta's story is about his by then favorite topic: racial exclusion. It contains an underlying critique of the Mexican character that refuses to accept otherness. *El huero*, as a gringo, is pushed to the margins of society. His culture will not allow him to find a tranquil space to live. In fact, this is a theme running through all of Zeta's oeuvre: the unassimilating attitude of Mexican-Americans in the United States. In *The Autobiography of a Brown Buffalo,* he claims he never dated Mexican girls in school "because they always stuck to themselves and refused to participate in the various activities." Racial exclusion and resistance began to take a fair amount of his attention. He was consciously shifting from a purely aesthetic to a more politically oriented approach to writing. The crossroads where the artist meets the activist was beginning to take shape in his heart.

Also part of his UCSB archives, "The Little House" is a sixteen-page story using characters and elements from *My Cart for My Casket,* and advancing what would later on become Zeta's autobiography. It tells the adventures of a young boy traveling with his mother on a Greyhound bus from El Paso to the little town of Burneyville in the San Joaquín Valley in search of his father. As soon as he arrives, he is rejected by a group of Mexican boys who deny him the right to play tag. Later on he finds a pretty girl, with whom he has a private conversation. The girl talks badly of her Mexican neighbors, who live in *el vario,* a Spanish word misspelled by Zeta throughout the text. "'Ah, they're just dumb Mexicans,' she said matter-of-factly, throwing the words off with an obvious tone. 'All the guys around here are a bunch of creeps,' she continued in the same tone, 'they think girls, Okies and new people are worse than cow shit.' She said that word as natural as if she used it every day of her life, which I wouldn't doubt if she did." Although structurally weak, this *cuento* is further evidence of Zeta's ambiguous identity: the boy likes the girl and wants to be with her. But when he hears her talk, he feels offended. What to do? Rather than pushing his protagonist to take a stand, Zeta leaves his reaction open, unresolved.

Other works of scholarly importance, written in San Francisco and Los Angeles respectively sometime after 1966, are the anarchic science fiction story "To Whom It May Concern" and *The Catalina Papers,* a two-act play. Subtitled "A Solicitation," the science fiction story is about a haunting escape of a father and his son from a global catastrophe. Two groups prevail in an end-of-time scene: *They* and *Us, Ellos* and *Nosotros.* Led by a Commander-in-Chief who addresses his constituency as ants, They are the forces of evil ready to torture and electrocute their opponents. As the narrative begins, the protagonist seems paralyzed. He is the last to leave the place where he now sits. A commotion—sirens, agitation—awaits him outside. He remembers his son. He rescues him, and the two run away, seeing blood and weapons everywhere. Suddenly, the narrative voice swifts from the first to the third person.

"Federico, be a big boy. A real big boy. Please," he implored as he held the cold pipe railing with one hand climbing down the steps leading to the wharf.

The boy reached his hand around his father's and said looking from around, "Why are we running, dad? is there a fire? Is that it, dad?" The boy almost cried begging for an answer.

"As soon as we get to the beach I'll tell you, son. Now we have to hurry. We're going to the beach. . . . You remember those caves we found by the bridge? . . . Remember that time we were fishing? . . ."

"But why so fast, dad? I don't see any fire engines or fire."

The boy touched the man's cheek. The man pressed his hand on the boy's hand and wanted to lick it.

Interestingly, the father is called Manuel, the name of Zeta's own dad, while the boy is Federico, the second name of Zeta's son. In the end, after a long persecution and with the father about to expire, he decides he cannot leave his son alive, and thus he takes out a knife and kills him. The story is designed to create empathy with his immolation. "Greater love has no man than to take another's life whom he loves." Similarly, *The Catalina Papers* is presented as a kind of totalitarian "experiment." It begins in the foyer of an auditorium in which each member of the audience must present his Social Security number. "No refreshments will be allowed," he writes. "No talking. No touching. A pencil and pad are given to each viewer. Uniformed guards will enforce the above rules." In essence, the play follows futuristic, semiscientific narrative lines. A Harvard-accented narrator talks about the plot to the audience, which supposedly consists of members of an encompassing institute:

> What you will see today are the effects of a process which gives the participants a different history, a temporary change in the memory banks. . . . In fact, most of you will recognize these specimens. . . . Each of them works in the Institute. . . . They will possess different characters and personalities, which were selected at random from the general population. The whole purpose of today's scenario is to demonstrate that man will subject himself to the experiment—that comes later; that given the conditions of total dependence as the sole means of survival, he will ultimately subject himself to the experiment of controller reproduction for purposes of perpetuation of the human race. But, frankly, you need not concern yourself

with the purpose of the experiment. . . . I've explained
simply to make it more meaningful to you.

Each of the characters in the play is asked to assume an
ethnic identity different from his or her own, the purpose
being to analyze the human response one is likely to get
when "living in somebody else's skin." Zeta introduces
apocalyptic elements: the protagonists feel they inhabit an
island à la Robinson Crusoe or, even better, William Gold-
ing's *Lord of the Flies.* They feel suffocated, anxious. As in
"To Whom It May Concern," the true value of the play lies
in its apocalyptic, anti-utopian vision. Increasingly, Zeta
found himself obsessed with the future. He wondered
what kind of tomorrow the racial miscegenation in the
United States would bring and was deeply concerned with
the government's increasing failure to control its citizens.
He felt inclined toward nineteenth-century theories of
utopian socialism, such as Prudhomme's and Bukharin's,
promoting the dissolution of the state. Politically, he would
write sometime later, "I believe in absolutely nothing. I
wouldn't lift a finger to fight anyone." He was an avid
reader of Konrad Lorenz's book-long essay, *On Aggression,*
which "impressed me as much as the Bible," and Robert
Ardrey's *The Territorial Imperative: A Personal Inquiry
into the Animal Origins of Property and Nations.* Man's
hostility, Zeta thought, was a natural thing, not a factor to
be ignored, avoided, or feared.

NO WAY, JOSÉ

Mexico, *lo mexicano*, was in Zeta's blood, in the food he ate, the music he detested, the California air he breathed. "I hate for people to assume I'm an authority on Mexicans," he once argued. "Just because I'm a Brown Buffalo doesn't mean I'm the son of Moctezuma." At the time he finished "Perla Is a Pig," he was more confident about himself. Suddenly a new identity seemed quite attainable. The story was simply signed: *Zeta*. His new appellation, his new persona "descended on him," *lo poseyó*, after he saw a Mexican revolutionary in a few old Hollywood movies. In his correspondence he mentions *The Mark of Zorro*, the 1921 version with Douglas Fairbanks. Elsewhere, he describes his sense of rejoice in watching Costa-Gavras's 1969 French art film, Z, about a political assassination in Greece, and he would become even more attached to the last letter of the alphabet. But the Zorro film is troublesome as a key to his enigmatic identity, simply because the mysterious hero fights a Mexican *canalla* to restore power to the Anglo establishment. Hispanics, as the critic Arthur G. Pettit has argued, are portrayed in it as a *mestizo* mobocracy. The plot is about Don Diego Vega, a Castilian *caballero* of impeccable pedigree. He poses in public as a dandy: He perfumes his hair, is a womanizer, and is at odds with his father, an aristocratic former governor of Spanish California. In his secret identity, Don Diego becomes Zorro—a black-clad masked hero with a flowing cape and a flashing blade who fights Mexicans to reinstate his father into the gubernatorial post. Zeta, attracted to the myth, took its larger significance and gave up its immediate political implications. A masked hero, a defender of the unfairly treated, a Robin Hood of quasi-Marxist views—he sympathized with the weight, the personality of the character. And in choosing his name, as well as the animal references (*búfalos* and *cucarachas*, buffaloes and cockroaches) to describe himself and his people, he also found inspiration elsewhere. "General Zeta was the hero of an old movie classic, *La Cucaracha*," he writes in a personal essay, "a combination of Zapata and Villa with María Félix as the femme fatale. It suits me just fine. And Brown Buffalo for the fat brown shaggy snorting American Animal, slaughtered almost to extinction." He ended by stating: "I feel right at home. . . ." Obviously the acquisition of another name symbolized reinventing himself. He could temporarily breach the abyss of his divided self, part Anglo and part Mexican, part English and part Spanish, by finding a new way to describe the hyphen, the in-between and undecided. As *Zeta,* as the outlaw, the *bandido,* he assumed the role of urban freedom fighter, of *el subversivo,* an anti-establishment figure. Racism, he now recognized, had been a constant ingredient in his upbringing and in his maturation process. He couldn't turn his back on injustice and discrimination. Hadn't he witnessed too much *cabronería* since childhood? *No, nunca jamás.* He was too belligerent, too self-possessed, too *hijo de puta,* too overwhelmed by the sins of society. He had to confront the powers that be and be honest with himself. Or didn't he? In *Zeta,* he finally heard his calling. This "name mask," he thought, should be expanded to the whole Chicano people. Mexican-Americans were not, would never be, like the rest of the U.S. citizenry. No way, José. They were a different nation, a people under occupation, an insular culture inhabiting the belly of an imperialist beast. "Who is the immigrant, Pilgrim?" asked a ubiquitous slogan of the era. The spirit of the times, let us not forget, encouraged sectarianism. The civil rights movement was well under way and the Reverend Martin Luther King, Jr., César Chávez, and other prominent black, Native American, and Hispanic leaders called attention to the inner contradictions of the American Dream. Not only was the United States attacking Vietnam, invading Southeast Asia, and disrupting Latin America. Its noxious tentacles also victimized its own underclass. Like many other *compañeros* enchanted with Ernesto "Ché" Guevara, Fidel Castro and the Cuban Revolution, Zeta wanted *la raza* to react, to be respected, to confront its aggressor. He called for a revolution within America.

The Chicanos—who were they? The original Aztecs, the People of the mythical Aztlán Aztlatan. Throughout his childhood and youth, Zeta knew of his Hispanic background. He was the victim of racism and discrimination. He traced his roots to Mexico. But he never investigated his

distant family's past. At least not intellectually. Now, all of a
sudden, the Chicano experience, his Mexican-American
ancestry, the history that defined and confused his identity,
passed before his eyes like an amazing dream in which one
plays the double role of observer and protagonist. History
as memory: a memory recalled, a memory that kept calling
him back in time—Zeta as part of La Raza; Zeta *el mexicano*; Zeta the Latino; Zeta as the quintessential *mestizo*.
Chicanos, he soon concluded, are Native Americans,
nativos with long roots in a past that precludes the
Mayflower. They are even proto-Mexicans in that, as the
legend claims, the original Aztecs began their nomadic
journey to Tenochtitlán in Aztlán, located somewhere in the
U.S. Southwest. The decisive historical moment: 1848, the
Treaty of Guadalupe Hidalgo, when parts of California,
Texas, Arizona, New Mexico, and other territories in northern Mexico were purchased by the Washington government, thus becoming part of *los estados unidos*. The Chicanos never moved, it was the world that moved around
them. Unlike other immigrant waves, they did not come to
the United States; the United States came to them.

Since the mid-nineteenth century, Mexican-American
history has been a sequel of misadventures in oppression,
victimization, and resistance: In 1910, a revolution lead by
Zapata and Villa south of the Rio Grande pushed many to
find asylum in the United States (between that year and
1912, nearly two thousand Mexicans crossed the border
every month to work for the railways); in 1916, Francisco
"Pancho" Villa, an "undesirable," is sought by the U.S. government; in 1920 the Johnson Act establishes strict limits

on immigrants from nations beyond the Western Hemisphere; in 1929 repatriation programs take place, and nearly 500,000 Mexicans (many of them U.S. citizens) are sent back over a five-year period; in 1942, the Sleepy Lagoon Incident in Los Angeles, in which twenty-four Chicano youths are charged with gang killings and seventeen are sentenced to prison until their convictions are reversed for lack of evidence and civil rights violations; a year later, the Zoot Suit Riots, in which U.S. servicemen attack Chicanos in Los Angeles, San Diego, Philadelphia, Chicago, and Detroit. Constant uproar, incessant transformation. In 1960 the Census Bureau declared Chicanos (referred to as Mexican-Americans) as the second largest minority population, reaching 3,842,000 nationally.[1] As a result of sheer numbers, they could not be dismissed anymore, and by the end of the decade, when Zeta was awakened to his heritage, the Chicano community had assumed a more active, vociferous stand. César Chávez changed things radically by organizing the National Farm Workers Association, which, through its grape strike, acquired international fame. Many urban Chicanos joined the strike, and soon a transient labor movement was transformed into *El Movimiento,* a fundamental aspect of the civil rights movement. Other important political figures in Denver, New Mexico, and Texas—such as Dolores Huerta, Reies López Tijerina, Rodolfo "Corky" González, and José Angel Gutiérrez—

---

[1]By 1990, the Census Bureau claimed there were 13.3 million (out of a total of around 22 million Hispanics), mostly based in the Southwest.

lead crusades for justice, orchestrated a 1970 moratorium, and organized the La Raza Unida party. *¡El desmadre!* The new Chicano identity was born.

During the sixties liaisons among Chicanos and other minority groups, like blacks and Native Americans, were established. Although he understood their political value, Zeta openly resented such partnerships. His work, particularly his autobiography, has been compared to that by black writers in the United States, especially *The Life and Times of Frederick Douglass,* the 1881 memoir by the runaway slave and later statesman, in that both narrators insist on reintegrating themselves into and speaking for their communities. Although true, my gut feeling is that such a comparison would have annoyed him. African-Americans were the largest minority when Zeta was active and, in the nation's consciousness, the most crucial. He consistently argued that guilt, *la culpa,* emerging from slavery made blacks the only "non-person" Anglos ever cared for; Chicanos, "real *indios,*" Puerto Ricans, and other minorities mattered very little. He resented the fact that his experience was always equated, always compared to that of blacks. He sympathized with others "whose civil rights have been turned into wrongs" but wanted individual, not collective, attention. Chicanos alone, *solos* and on their own right—that's what he sought! While he identified with the term "Chicano," he preferred Brown Buffaloes, *Bisons americanus*: members of a large herd "that everyone slaughters," indigenous rather than foreign, virtually extinct. When united in a stampede, Mexican-Americans, he thought, could collectively struggle to destroy their oppressor. Once, when fired from the public defender's office, he wondered if "what they really fired me for was my name: Buffalo Zeta Brown." And by addressing Chicanos as cockroaches, defined by *The American Heritage Dictionary* as "any of various oval, flat-bodied insects of the family Blattidæ, several species of which are common household pests," he endorsed the idea of belonging to a clan of "despicable insects." In his autobiography, he writes in a candid, slick fashion about his newly acquired identity:

Ladies and gentlemen . . . my name is Oscar Acosta. My father was an Indian from the mountains of Durango. Although I cannot speak his language . . . you see, Spanish is the language of our conquerors . . . English is the language of our conquerors. . . . No one ever asked me or my brother if we wanted to be American citizens. We are all citizens by default. They stole our land and made us half-slaves. They destroyed our gods and made us bow down to a dead man who's been strung up for 2,000 years. . . . Now what we need is, first to give ourselves a new name. We need a new identity. A name and a language all our own. . . . So I propose that we call ourselves . . . what's this, you don't want me to attack your religion? Well, all right. . . . I propose we call ourselves the Brown Buffalo people. . . . No, it's not an Indian name, for Christ sake . . . don't you get it? The buffalo, see? Yes, the animal that everyone slaughtered. . . . Sure, both the cowboys and the Indians are out to get him . . . and, because we do have roots in our Mexican past, our Aztec ancestry, that's where we get the brown from. . . .

Not without reason, he frequently enjoyed singing to himself "the old revolutionary song" of the 1910 Mexican social trifle that stands as "the only Spanish I know":

> *La cucaracha, la cucaracha,*
> *Ya no puede caminar.*
> *Porque le falta,*
> *Porque le falta,*
> *Marijuana pa'fumar.*

Acosta *and* Zeta: one inside the other, one in spite of the other. This name game pinpoints a much deeper channel in Zeta's labyrinthine soul. It makes me think of Sh. Y. Abramovitch, the so-called grandfather of Yiddish letters, who, by means of his pseudonym, created a new persona in his literary work, Mendele Mokher Sforim, one different from his own personality. The dialectical relationship between Zeta's person and persona emerge from his character Brown Zeta Buffalo, featured in *The Revolt of the Cockroach People.* Read attentively, every single piece of fiction and autobiography by Zeta has him as the sole protagonist. Both his published books are about his heroic adventures, and the last book he was drafting before his death also deals with his own ego. He used literature to investigate his duality, his hyphenated self. And Zeta, while a pen name, was also a mask, a disguise. By becoming *Zeta,* a *bandido,* he inserted himself in the annals of Chicano history as a fanciful, enchanting character, a sane Don Quixote. He became a *rebelde con causa.* His political cause would soon take over every sphere, from the domes-

tic to the public. Sometime in mid-August 1970, for example, while traveling in Washington, he sent a postcard to
his son. "Moskito," it read. "Washington is not my father.
He took the land from our people. Power to the People!
Z." Aztlán was his only parentage, not the *Mayflower.* He
was a Mexican in America, not an American of Mexican
descent. In an untitled text found in his archives, he wrote:

My name is Zeta. I have read that the letter-name has
numerous strange meanings, derivatives from ancient
gods and inscribed in stone tablets rising skyward into
foggy mists. It is also the sixth letter of the Greek alphabet and the last of the Spanish. It is also the same letter
used to write the name of the famous brand of toilet
paper, viz., *Zee.* I once saw a movie called Z—in downtown El Paso, to be exact—with a French fag, about the
politics of Greece, etc. They said it meant, "He shall
return." It is the most beautiful of the letters in the
American alphabet. Also the easiest and the most dra-
matic of them all to actually scribble down on a piece of
paper—on the temple's door. . . . And, of course, we
mustn't forget our old friend: *Zorro,* and his little chili-
bean sidekick. Call me Zeta. It is a name of historical pro-
portion. A name to be reckoned with.

THE BOMB EXPLODES

His limited knowledge of *el español* is subject to debate. Throughout his work he gave conflicting accounts of his fluency, both oral and written. His father had forced him and his siblings to switch to English at an early age, and he felt nostalgic about its loss. How much did he remember? Marco, Anita, Hunter Thompson, and others claim he was well equipped to speak it. "In Mexican restaurants south of the Rio Grande," his son told me, "he would talk a mile a minute with waiters. Whenever we were in Mexico, he would always use his Spanish. Probably he didn't sound as a native speaker, but he knew what was going on." His sister claims Zeta "enjoyed deceiving people about his fluency. He would make you think he didn't know a word, when in fact he understood everything you and everybody else had said." The UCSB archives, on the other hand, evidence a Zeta never in full control of Cervantes's tongue.

And Mexico, was he ever south of the border for long stays? He spent a fair amount of time south of the border with his second wife, Socorro, a UCLA student originally from Michoacán to whom Zeta got married *en tierras de Cuauhtémoc,* after driving away in his parents' Cadillac. Indeed, Mexico always figured prominently in the map of his imagination. He probably first visited *la madre patria,* Mexico, on his way to Panama in the early fifties. After his marriage to Socorro Aguiniga (he divorced her in 1971), he traveled back, together with Marco, in the summer of 1969. They first went to Aspen, where they stayed with Hunter Thompson, then to Texas, Ciudad Juárez, and finally to Mexico City. The trip was three months long. Marco recalls his father being very dynamic, verbal, even aggressive. He would carry guns and knives. The two were accompanied by Frank Vega, a friend and later on Zeta's bodyguard in the 1970 campaign for sheriff of Los Angeles County. The journey ended in Acapulco, where they all stayed with one Jesus. Marco recalls living with almost no money. One night, while staying in a cheap hotel in Mexico City, he remembers his father waking him and Frank up around midnight. He had had a fight with the hotel owner, who wanted to charge him more than he was ready to pay. He had decided to sneak out through the back door without paying his bill. That's the type of life they would often lead: as fugitives, *bandidos,* outlaws always without sleep.

Another crucial journey, in October 1972, during the McGovern-Nixon presidential election, had two clear-cut purposes: to finish *The Revolt of the Cockroach People* and to find the whereabouts of his brother, Robert. Identified as Bob in *The Autobiography of a Brown Buffalo,* he was Zeta's most decisive childhood model and source of inspiration, as well as the family's troublemaker. He passed away in April 1990 and is buried in Mexicali. Some background: Since very young, Bob, a big-chested man and a real *cabrón*, had a chronic problem with alcohol, drugs, and crime. In an insightful letter to a certain Judge Bush, dated December 17, 1964, and written in San Francisco, Zeta, assuming his double role as brother and lawyer, writes: "Roberto Acosta of Modesto has been in trouble with the law for the past ten years, the violations ranging from common drunk to narcotics. If one were to merely consider the offenses and their repetition no one would question the necessary repercussions of a long jail sentence. It is in fact the position the entire family had taken following his most recent crime. After ten years of giving and trying without a single sign of rehabilitation the family concluded that 'Maybe jail is the best thing.'" Zeta offers some details about Bob's education. He claims his brother was a model student and a responsible human being with a wonderful future ahead of him. "We were not really aware of his truly broken condition." But in the summer of 1957, "he ran from drunkenness to a Mexico marriage and the inevitable divorce. He neither worked nor studied for any length. His friends from school and even his family finally after several years tired of his behavior and his new associates in crime." Zeta claimed Bob needed psychiatric therapy, but, instead, was sentenced to the San Bruno prison, and when he was set free, he was much sicker. "He was less of a human being and more of a criminal as a direct result of his incarceration without medical treatment." Zeta asks Judge Bush not to repeat the mistake: to offer him humane treatment, not the punishment of jail. "Hav-

ing studied the law for four years has led me to believe that
the law is what a judge will do with certain facts." What
Robert needs, he claims, is a sense of humanity, because
without mercy "he will in all probability continue the life
he has lived the past ten years. This may be our last opportunity and his last chance." What's important about the letter is its prophetic component. Zeta himself has danced on
the edge of the law. As time goes by, his daily existence will
be complicated by outbursts of fury, fights with the police
and judges, and his involvement in drug trafficking. In a
sense, Bob is Zeta's mirror, an extreme personification of
an important facet of his own character he has trouble controlling. Although they kept on fighting, he loved his older
brother more than anything else. In a note to him written
after a huge discussion, he recollects affectionately: "Bob,
Wale sandwiches at three in the P.M. Chasing dragons
down Jackson Street. Midge Magota pissing in the salad.
And you and me with the pipe up our butts. . . . Truce,
Zeta."

Around that time Bob had been working for a state-run
antipoverty program in San Francisco. One day, in mid-
1972, he ran away with some $20,000 and his four-year-old
son, Emiliano, named after Zapata. He crossed the Rio
Grande. The Feds and the Mexican police, as well as Bob's
second wife, Katty McCarthy, were after him. When they
finally found him, badly beaten, his bones broken, one
of his legs swollen (he had gone from weighing about
180 pounds to around 110), the angered mother took
Emiliano back to the United States, but left her husband
behind. Bewildered, with the excuse of finding "a quiet

place" to write, Zeta and his son, Marco, set out to "save him." Although tortured in Morelia, they located Bob in Mazatlán, where he was with René, a new girlfriend. First they transported him to a small, shadowy hotel room. Then they placed him in one of the Freeman Apartments, where he got into shape and decided to return home to turn himself in. He ended up with a one-year sentence at Terminal Island, a minimum security prison in Southern California.

Actually, Bob had a more active role to play in Zeta's odyssey. Thanks to him Zeta came to recognize his *destino manifiesto*. In Zeta's eyes his brother would always have an aura of sanctity. *The Autobiography of a Brown Buffalo* concludes with Zeta and his brother in a tête-à-tête. Lost and confused, the attorney wanted to get some money from him to finance an excursion to Guatemala in which he wants to channel weapons to guerrilla freedom fighters. His brother tells him he is broke and unable to help. But he suggests a better idea, to travel to East Los Angeles to write an article about the La Raza movement shaping in the area. Zeta confesses not to have heard a single thing about this internal insurrection. He has never heard the term "Brown Power." His brother tells him that a riot, organized by a group called the Brown Berets, is going to happen *muy pronto*. Something to do with school strikes and walkouts. "Why not go down there and write about *that* revolution, sell the story and *then* go to Guatemala?" asked Bob. Zeta is suddenly overwhelmed with joy. "The bomb explodes in my head. Flashes of lightning. Stars in my eyes. I see it all before me. That is exactly what the gods have in store for me. Of course, why didn't I think of it first? I thank him, I praise him and I beg him to send me fifty bucks immediately. I will take the Greyhound to Los Angeles, call my cousin Manuel and have him put me up for a few days until I get the story from, who'd you say, the Brown Berets? God damn, why didn't I think of that?"

Thus, Bob helped Zeta see the light. His true role, he finally understood, was to defend *a los miserables*, the poor. Actually, his passion for the underdog harks back to his decision to apply to law school. He wanted to understand the legal system in order to subvert it. Consequently, he would become a lawyer. It was the early sixties when Zeta began studying at night at San Francisco Law School. After much struggle, he passed the California State Bar Exam in June 1966, in his second try after failing the test the previous August. He proudly showed his parents the certificate. "I'm finally somebody," he wrote in a diary. As an attorney his activities began in the East Oakland Legal Aid Society, an antipoverty agency some eighty miles away from Modesto. Although he never had enough clients, the job was mentally exhausting. He was exposed to human suffering, and once again his emotional stability was put in question. Could he handle what he saw? Could he become *el mesías de los miserables*, a poor people's messiah? Inadvertently, his final journey, his descent into hell, had begun.

He quit his Oakland legal job on July 1, 1967, and escaped in a green '65 Plymouth. As he puts it, he's "escaping" and declares the occasion a day of rebellion: He gives up his job, fires his psychiatrist, and leaves his life and friends in San Francisco. His resignation, described at the beginning of *The Autobiography of a Brown Buffalo,* has been read by many Latino intellectuals as a call to arms, an acknowledgment of the pen as the best sword to fight injustice and poverty. I remember talking about it not long ago with Martín Espada, the Puerto Rican *independentista* poet based in Amherst, Massachusetts, responsible for the book *City of Coughing and Dead Radiators.* He described to me how when he read Zeta's account, he was mesmerized and found himself crying. He had also worked for a tenant lawyer in Boston for several years, and Zeta showed him the way from the legal profession into literature.

Zeta picked up Karin Wilmington, who had been hitchhiking despite being wealthy. Without a clear destination, he followed her to Idaho, where he would meet, at a bar and coffeehouse in Ketchum, Mike Solheim, the man who would introduce him to Hunter S. Thompson. He experimented with drugs and the limits of freedom. He also assumed new "ethnic" identities: at one point, he called himself Henry Hawk; playing out people's assumptions of his skin color and background, he asserted a Samoan heritage; or he claimed to be a Blackfoot Indian from Oklahoma. His journey of self-discovery, full of cocaine-eating parties, LSD in aspirin bottles, and tear gas raids on friendly bars, also took him to a pantheon of literary heroes. Among his first stops, in Ketchum in 1967, was Hemingway's grave, where he fell asleep. He moved frenetically from place to place, from one experience to another, until he arrived, without a car, at El Paso, where he was born, "to see if I could find the object of my quest. I still wanted to know who in the hell I really was." He revisited his past and reevaluated the Mexican presence in the U.S.-Mexican border. "With a cold wind at my back I scoured the neighborhood of my youth. It was just a stone's throw from the border. Crackling, rusty electric street cars, Mexican restaurants and bars blaring *norteño* music onto gutted, packed, crowded sidewalks teeming with brown faces, black hair and that ancient air of patience which I'd always seen in the faces of the *indio* from the mountains of Durango. I saw Mexican people with brown, wrapped packaged, paper bags filled with groceries, and mattened straw shopping bags of green, brown and red. They waited for streetcars with their *mandado* in hand."

In early 1968 Zeta found himself in a jail in Ciudad Juárez. He had entered into a fight after insulting a hotel clerk and was arrested. The police stripped him of his clothes and searched for knives and dope. They mistreated him. He explained to them he was not a Mexican citizen but *un americano*. To no avail. At one point, he was brought in front of a judge. Zeta tried to defend himself. He said he didn't have his Bar license with him. Again, the issue of looks is crucial. "I know I don't exactly *look* like an attorney . . . but you see, the hair styles are no longer in San Francisco . . . no, of course I'm not a hippie, I'm an attorney at law, your honor. . . ." He considered bribing the judge, but wondered: "I, an attorney, a citizen of the United States, should I become a partner to the corruption of justice in my very own father's country?"

Self-discovery turned into a trap. Every mirror distorted his image. He was looking for light but could find only darkness. Darkness outside. A heart of darkness. A

thousand questions, a thousand doubts—but only evasive
answers. Finally, on a rainy day in January, either by sheer
accident or as a result of his endless deadlocks, some clue
came to him: Identity was the enigma and ethnicity was
the solution. "My single mistake," he concluded, "has been
to seek an identity with any one person or nation or with
any part of history." He added: "What I see now . . . , what
is clear to me after this sojourn is that I am neither a Mexican nor an American. I am neither a Catholic nor a Protes-
tant. I am a Chicano by ancestry and a Brown Buffalo by
choice."

Zeta's most explosive period began after his rendezvous
in El Paso, when he traveled to California, a state he first
visited at age five, and ended up in Los Angeles, a city that
in his eyes was too chaotic, schizophrenic, extremely violent. He stayed in "sleazy downtown hotels." His view was
depressing. He wrote in *The Revolt of the Cockroach People*: ". . . already my bones have told me that I have come
to the most detestable city on earth. They have carried me
through the filthy air of a broken city filled with battered
losers. Winos in tennis, skinny fags in tight pants and
whores in purple skirts all ignore the world beyond the
local bar, care about nothing except where the booze
comes cheapest or the latest score on the radio. Where I
am, the buildings are crumbling into pieces. The paint is
cracked and falling to the street covered with green and
brown phlegm, with eyeless souls who scuttle between tall
buildings hoping to find a bed, a bottle, a joint, a board or
even a loaf of bread. . . ."

He contrasted barrio life with the affluence of Bel Air

and Malibu. The guys he identified with were *vatos locos,*
in Raymund A. Paredes's definition, "descendants of the
pachuco, the zoot-suited rebel of the 1940s and 1950s"
who "is found [at the time] in virtually all urban areas with
a substantial Chicano population." He referred to them as
cockroaches, *rascuache* people who live in squalor and are
reviled by others of higher economic status and admired
for their disdain for Anglo values.

He told people in Los Angeles he was writing an article
for the *New York Times* about the Chicano upheaval. He
enjoyed portraying himself as a disoriented out-of-town
boy stunned by an electrifying atmosphere. "Education, not
Eradication!" stated one banner. "Fences Are for Criminals
and Animals!" "Put Chicanos in Our History Books!" "Chicano Power Today and Forever!" "Yankees Out of Aztlán!"
But, as he states in his writing, he deeply resented the fact
that Chicano political activities were often delegated to the
back pages of the city's and the nation's dailies. The
imagery of the Brown Buffalo and the Cockroach People
become even closer to his heart. His entrance to the theater of Chicano history was extremely timely. Almost as
soon as he arrived, he had his business card made: BUF-
FALO Z. BROWN, CHICANO LAWYER, BELMONT HOTEL, L.A.
He began walking hand in hand with personalities like
César Chávez, whom he paid a personal visit. As his
involvement deepens, he shared the stage with Angela
Davis and Rodolfo "Corky" González, the militant poet
responsible for *I Am Joaquín/Yo Soy Joaquín,* whom Zeta
always preferred in contrast to César Chávez. He was
asked to represent thirteen Chicano militants indicted by

the Los Angeles County grand jury on charges of conspiracy to disrupt the public schools. As a poverty, civil rights,
people's lawyer who represented East L.A. Chicanos, Zeta
saw himself as a north-of-the-border proletarian hero. He
defended the poor and hoped to take something away
from the rich: power and oppressive authority. He was an
outspoken critic of racism and anti-Mexican feeling.

A famous case, chronicled in *The Revolt of the Cockroach People,* involved Robert Fernández, a teenager
found dead in his cell at the East L.A. sheriff's substation.
Fernández allegedly hanged himself while in prison, but
Zeta and the young man's family, who asked the coroner's
office to conduct an autopsy, suspected he died of a beat-
ing by police. At first the coroner hesitated, but he
accepted with the stipulation that Zeta must be present at
the autopsy. The spectacle was terrifying: He watched the
way in which the young Chicano was literally cut into
pieces, and chunks of his neck, face, and chest were
hacked. The autopsy was declared inconclusive, but the
lesson was powerful: Zeta had watched a cockroach treated
"like shit" by the Anglo establishment.

He also defended various Chicano protest groups and
activists such as the St. Basil 21 and "Corky" González himself. Although incomplete, the files at UCSB offer some
insight into his lawsuits. He defended two Brown Berets
charged with felonies stemming from the 1969 disruption
of a speech by then Governor Ronald Reagan at the Biltmore Hotel. He was also involved in attempts to change
education in California and was active defending Hispanics
against discrimination. That led him to be in a few impor-

tant cases, many of which are detailed in *The Revolt of the Cockroach People*. In *Castro v. Los Angeles*, he represented Salvatorre Castro, a high school teacher who had been indicted on charges arising out of high school walkouts protesting low standards of education. As Zeta described it in his work, Castro and his colleagues had been charged with felony conspiracy and charged with disrupting the peace in various schools. As a lawyer, he won a decision that involved constitutional First Amendment rights. As the critic Joe D. Rodríguez details, the California State Court of Appeals ruled that the felony conspiracy charges be squashed because stricter standards of proof were necessary to protect First Amendment rights. Zeta was also the leading lawyer in the case *Carlos Montes et al. v. Los Angeles County*, in which he fought to show that Mexican-American citizens, particularly those with clear Spanish surnames, had been discriminated from participating in the Los Angeles County grand jury.

Often plagued with anachronisms and erroneous information, Zeta's narrative account of the overall civil rights turmoil offers a window to the turmoil of the time and a door into his own mental state. "All through law school," he wrote in *The Revolt of the Cockroach People*, "my secret dream had been to work with Chávez and the *campesinos*. . . . My fantasies ran to the vineyards and orchards at César's side, a union organizer rather than a courtroom attorney." He became ever more radical as his legal experience increased. A sense of loyalty and community with *mi gente* was evident in his behavior. The unhappiness that surrounded him in the Oakland antipoverty

agency had vanished: He was a man with a mission and a
sense of duty. *Un campeón.* He would write letters to a
judge complaining against discrimination, and he even
composed a fascinating essay, entitled "Challenging Racial
Exclusion on the Grand Jury," written in 1969, which
detailed his strategy in the case of *East L.A. 13 v. Los
Angeles Supreme Court.* Published in a small law school
news service, *Caveat,* the author is identified as "Attorney
Oscar Zeta Acosta." The essay opens with an editor's note
in italics: "The *Caveat* is indebted to Attorney Acosta of
the Mexican-American Legal Defense and Educational
Fund for permission to print this important and provocative article. Proud of his heritage, Oscar Zeta details . . .
the exclusion of Spanish-speaking people from the Grand
Jury in Los Angeles over the years. The situation in L.A. is
only a manifestation of the problem throughout California,
and Attorney Acosta points out the growing militance of
the young Chicanos who will no longer tolerate injustice
anywhere." Zeta began by describing the growth of the
Mexican-American community in Los Angeles County,
"the largest ethnic minority in America's largest county,"
and accused the government of ignoring their civil rights.
"Once the owners and possessors of this City of Angeles,"
he wrote, "this 'Spanish Surnamed' peoples with an unique
proximity to their original homelands—only three hours to
Mexico by Greyhound—continue to increase at twice the
rate of the Anglo majority throughout the entire Southwest
where, in one fast and furious year, they have without
precedent adopted a nationalistic, militant posture all their
own with a zeal and cry the Anglo assumed had died, if not

with the grant of citizenship under the treaty of Guadalupe Hidalgo, at least with Zapata." He proceeds to describe the events of March 1968, when Chicano teachers boycotted and walked out of their schools. "We Are Not Dirty Mexicans!" one banner stated in Los Angeles. "Uncle Sam Stole Our Land!" "The myth of the passive Mexican," Zeta continued, "blew up in this anxious city's poisonous air as waves of mini-skirted, brown-skinned, black-haired girls echoed in tandem the angry, clenched-fist cry of these new Machos in the barrios: *Viva La Raza!* Chicano Power! Education—not eradication! These were the new *gritos,* the young, brown radicals (sporting cocky brown berets and khaki field-jackets) exhorted their poverty-ridden, black-eyed *Camaradas* to yell to the *Gabacho* [gringo] as they marched to the School Board with their proposals previously hammered-out at ubiquitous community meetings over a six-month period."

He commented how, after the March walkouts, most Chicano leaders and students had been granted amnesty—except the East L.A. 13, who were indicted on fifteen counts of conspiracy to disrupt the public schools, felonies punishable by up to forty-five years in state prisons. He then explained that "in Los Angeles County, the Grand Jurors are nominated by the Superior Court Judges. Over a ten-year period, 178 judges nominated a total of 1,501 nominees, of which only twenty were Spanish surnamed. Of these judges, 91.6% never once nominated a Spanish-surnamed person. The actual Grand Juror is then selected at random from the list of nominees, and, understandably, the result has been a mere token representation of *all* the minorities. Specifically, only four (4) out of a total of 210 Grand Jurors, or 1.9%, has been a person with a Spanish Surname, and one of these is in fact a Negro." He concluded that racial exclusion was prohibited in jury selection as early as the Civil Rights act of 1875, continued to accuse the state of discrimination, and ended with what can be read as an early diagnosis on the Chicano Movement: "What about the Chicano revolutionaries?" he asked.

It is much too early to say in what direction their nationalism will travel; too soon to even suggest that their actions will be governed by the society's response to their claims for equality. The concepts of integration, assimilation and acculturation describe historical relationships between Africans, Orientals and Europeans, persons all foreign to this land. Despite the lack of organization or of truly national leaders, despite the inability to articulate his rage, the Mexican-American claims the Southwest by right of prior possession, by right of ancestry. His most distinctive, prominent characteristic is his *Indio-Mestizo* blood; that is the deeper meaning of *La Raza*. And whether we speak of historical or Einsteinian time, it *was* but a few moons ago that this Southwest was inhabited exclusively by the Indians. One thing is certain, this we can say: The Mexican will not perish for lack of dreams; for whatever the outcome, the young Chicano presently dreams of Zapata while reading his Ché.

As a lawyer he was often broke. Broke and outraged. At one point, he was invited to speak at UCLA about Chicano activism, but he was distressed and disappointed to find an audience of affluent students lacking true political commitment. When local organizers for a presidential candidate donated $10,000 to the activists' defense fund in order to win Chicano votes, their check bounced. He lived in an age of injustice and silence. But he was ready to speak out: *gritar o morir.*

Known for his bad temper in court, for screaming at judges and not controlling his behavior, his license was often in jeopardy. But Zeta couldn't care less. He didn't want to lose the outspoken, flamboyant spirit. It was an essential part of his personality, his authentic *yo me[ch][x]icano.* Take as a symptomatic example a letter to him by a defendant, Luis Talamantez, in the San Quentin Prison, written in August 1971. Talamantez accused Zeta of failing to prepare the legal documents for his defense. He had not shown up at agreed-upon meetings and had apparently received money from questionable sources. In short, the attorney had abandoned the case without any notice. "You were recently telephoned upon my request," wrote Talamantez. "Your response as related to me was both sad and disheartening. You state that you are not functioning nor feel willing to work on case matters needing your attention because you haven't any money. As a peoples lawyer you'll not ever be endowed with the monetary sums by which to assist you to reach the extents of your given commitment and entrusted responsibilities. I expect you to struggle on, nevertheless. . . ." He concluded in a more frank way: "Oscar, in all sincerity please reevaluate your commitment as my lawyer. I expect more from

you. You will either have to get a lot more serious and work
to overcome a lot of this shit or you'll have to withdraw. I
like you, *Vato*. . . . I ain't going to put up with any of this
negative type shit though, *entiendes?* Do something."

A couple of months later, on November 16, 1971, the
Los Angeles Times reported that Zeta was giving up the
practice of law. "Acosta, well known both for his fiery
defense of militant Mexican-Americans and his courtroom
verbal battles with judges, said he now lives in Modesto
and is going to devote his time to writing." And then, of
course, was the issue of his drug addiction. A *Herald
Examiner* news clip from August 28, 1971, states that
"Oscar Acosta, 36, defense lawyer for 10 Mexican-Americans being tried on charges of setting fires at the Biltmore
Hotel, today was arrested by undercover agents in Hollywood and held on a booking of possession of dangerous
drugs." He would later be freed on a $1,250 bail, but the
incident marks Zeta's public persona at the time: frequently under arrest, explosive, uncontrollable.

WHY NOT, *HOMBRE?*

Zeta reached a vociferous apex as an attorney in the early seventies. He wanted a more active role in *la revolución.* *Ser un heroe,* a more prominent stand alongside other luminaries of The New Nation of Aztlán. To achieve more recognition, he devised a sophisticated strategy: He would attract more media attention, when possible would behave even more outrageously, and more important, he would run for public office under an independent platform. His party would be La Raza Unida. Written on his personal stationery displaying an Aztec letter style, his press release dated February 23, 1970, from his home, 5327 East Beverly Boulevard, in Los Angeles, declaring his candidacy for sheriff of Los Angeles County (population: 7,000,000), asked acquaintances to support him in his political career. "The history of Los Angeles County is one of violence, vice and corruption in high places," he wrote.

Neither the expenditure of huge sums of money nor an increase in the personnel of all the law enforcement

agencies throughout the county has diminished the decay
inherent in our communities. On the contrary, history is
replete with examples to prove that the privilege of bearing
guns and their use under color of law has in all probability
increased the incidence of violence. There can therefore
be no justification for the continued waste of millions of
taxpayers dollars in the maintenance of the militia within
the confines of the county. Because the forces of oppression and suppression—the law enforcement agencies—
continue to harass, brutalize, illegally confine and psycho-
logically damage the Chicano, the Black, the poor and the
unrepresented, I hereby declare my candidacy for the
office of Sheriff of Los Angeles County.

He added:

I would like to interest you in working for our campaign for
The People. I am convinced that we are in the final years
of a relatively peaceful society, that the next few campaigns
will be the final gasp before all hell breaks loose throughout the country and indeed throughout the world. The present form of governments on the national, state and local
level seem totally inadequate to meet the needs of the citizenry. Political parties and labels have become meaningless
and irrelevant to the issues that plague our society. Struc-
tures, philosophies, ideologies, rules of law and procedure
are simply not working and it is apparent to me that they
will no longer work in a society such as we have created in
between our numerous wars. It seems to me that if we are
to survive the holocaust of imminent degradation and

destruction, that we must prepare now for a structure, a way of life that might hopefully turn back the tide.

He suggested that he was not running for sheriff out of greed or personal ambition but because nobody else seemed to be suited for the job.

Zeta first announced his political intentions to the legendary Rubén Salazar, a radio announcer and a *Los Angeles Times* reporter, in the KMEX radio interview in 1970. The topic of the interview was one of Zeta's legal cases, his defense of the family of Robert Fernández. During their dialogue, Zeta addressed Chicanos as *Las Cucarachas* and blamed the L.A. County sheriff for the brutality against Mexican-Americans in his prisons. Salazar was puzzled:

"'Cockroach' you say, Mr. Brown?"

"Yeah, the Cockroach People . . . you know, the little beasts that everyone steps on."

"Heh, heh . . . I see. . . . And, uh, so you think the Sheriff was engaged in this killing. Sheriff Peter Peaches?"[1]

"Not personally . . . but he is responsible for his men. He's the boss. . . . When I get in there, I'll see to it that those who are guilty are punished."

"When you get in there?"

"Yes, I have decided that the job is too important to be left to killer dogs like Peter Peaches."

[1] In the "interview" that appears in *Revolt of the Cockroach People*, Acosta slightly changed the names of some people to avoid legal problems. Sheriff Peter Peaches is Pete Pritchess; Mr. Zanzibar is Ruben Salazar.

"Are you trying to say that you're going to run for Sheriff?"

"Yeah. You got yourself a scoop, Mr. Zanzibar. I just filed for the office before I came down to the station. . . . Here, this is my receipt for the filing fee."

He told Salazar his campaign would have one single issue: education. "I know there's no hope for actual victory at the ballot box. I have no money and no supporters other than a few ragged friends. We can hardly compete with the pros." He wanted to be elected in order to disband the Los Angeles police force. "The police are the violent arm of the rich," he would say, "and I would get rid of them." The candidacy statement ended with a few slogans: "No man can tell another how, or even if he should be free. . . . Do Your Own Thing! *Justicia y Libertad.*" He pledged the ultimate dissolution of the sheriff's department; the interim actual and symbolic demilitarization of deputies; the immediate withdrawal of concentrated forces in the barrios and ghettos; the immediate investigation into criminal activities of law enforcement officers; the implementation of community review boards from the various areas; the immediate use of personnel, equipment, and facilities for utilitarian and socially beneficial programs as recommended and approved by community review boards; and equality of treatment and justice for all.

He often appeared in newspapers and was active proclaiming the need to include Hispanics in politics. He wrote a letter to the Chicano community, addressing it as "Estimada Raza," in which he explained his reasons for continuing in politics while accusing Richard Nixon and Ronald Reagan of killing social programs and thus attacking Mexican-Americans. I quote:

Mi opinión es que la presente revolución sólo tendrá éxito cuando dejemos de engañarnos de que todavía hay esperanza de sobrevivir en este sistema racista. La esperanza que nos da la Ayuda Legal es un paso en dirección equivocada. A pesar de las buenas intenciones de los "gabachos" liberales que nos defienden a su manera, estoy convencido que ultimadamente estamos mejor cuando la Ayuda Legal, y otros programas del Gobierno, se salgan del barrio. Si debemos sufrir, hagámoslo solos, sin miedo y con la dignidad de los que prefieren libertad a limosnas. Si estos "gabachos" liberales estuvieran seriamente trabajando para La Raza, tomando órdenes de La Raza, y realmente haciendo algo de valor, tal vez mi conclusión fuera distinta . . . pero la realidad es que todavía nos ven como "los prietitos" que necesitan su ayuda y actúan como los patroncitos de ayer—arrogantes y paternalistas. Raza: A pesar de los constantes chismes sobre mi personalidad y amistad, me presento ante ustedes como cualquier soldado que ha aprendido a tomar lecciones del pasado. Estoy listo a tomar órdenes de mi comunidad de La Raza Unida.

I translate:

My opinion is that the present revolution will only succeed when we stop fooling ourselves that there's still hope to survive in this racist system. The hope provided by the

Legal Help is a step in the wrong direction. In spite of
the good intentions by the liberal gringos, who defend us
in their own way, I am convinced that, ultimately, we are
better off when Legal Help and other social programs
provided by the government leave our barrio. If we need
to suffer, let us do so alone, without fear and with the dig-
nity of those who prefer freedom to charity. If these liberal gringos were really working on the behalf of La Raza,
taking orders from La Raza, doing something worthwhile,
my opinion would probably be different. But actually, we
are still seen as "the little brown people," who need their
help, making them act as old patrons—in an arrogant and
paternalistic fashion. Raza: In spite of the constant
rumors surrounding my personality and friendships, I
present myself to you as a common soldier who has
learned the lessons of the past. I am ready to take orders
from my community, La Raza Unida.

Several times his desire to continue campaigning was
governed by doubt. He had become well known in the
state media and was often quoted and misquoted on
numerous issues. He entered the race with the certainty
that a victory would never come, no matter what. Almost
simultaneously, Jesús Colón, the Puerto Rican activist and
writer, ran for the office of comptroller, and Norman
Mailer and Jimmy Breslin ran for mayor of the city of New
York. Zeta ensured a few endorsements, including one
from a political organization in Los Angeles County known
as the Congress of Mexican-American Unity. But in the
following months, he was anxious. He had trouble with

many judges, his enemies had multiplied like mushrooms after the rain, and more than anything else, he was heavily addicted to powerful drugs. At one point, he sent a letter to Willie L. Brown, Jr., a prominent California legislator who had graduated from law school at the same time Zeta had and was a candidate in another election. "I have, after several days of consideration, decided to write to you explaining why I will no longer be a part of the campaign," he claimed. What follows serves as a window for understanding Zeta as politician and artist.

> The hesitancy was based primarily on the fear of being considered presumptuous, however, on reconsideration, I concluded that neither of us being the exclusive possessors of wisdom the letter might be beneficial to both of us; for me, the writing would more clearly bring my reasoning into focus, and for you, that you might know of my position and for your own career try to understand it.
>
> As you know, I am but a babe in political activity. I've not experienced the chagrin that undoubtedly follows unsuccessful activity thereby creating cynicism, or the belief in political expediency as the best means to accomplish the desired goal. Being practical has never appealed to me. I have been a creature of the arts for too long. Truth and beauty have been more desirable than achievement. I do not mean to say that goals of power should be sacrificed on the altar of truth, or better, power through truth, as opposed to the achievement of power by means of practical politics, which is, to me, a distortion of truth.
>
> As a lawyer you will probably more rapidly appreciate

the facts rather than an exposition of my ideals. But the facts are difficult to find. As I look back upon the past months to find exactly what it is that displeased me, that caused me to make this decision, it is not easy, the exact words elude me. As I restate them they sound petty. They are as if from the mind of a child. It seems, at times as this, that being practical is maybe a more mature position. I know I have mentioned some of these things to others and they've looked at me with that mocking eye, or what I mistook for such, and said, "Come on, man!"

Nevertheless, here are a few.

I am against discrimination . . . all of it. You say you are too. . . . Yet you speak of the white and the non-white vote. What you really mean is the Negro and the non-Negro vote. You are spending the majority of your time, money and labor on the Negro vote. You will continue to do the same until June.

How about those of us who are neither white nor non-white? That is, who shall represent those of us who are neither Negro nor white?

There are too many people in this world who view life this way. No one ever really thought that Lincoln or the Civil War cleared the mess up, but those of us with sufficient intelligence, awareness and sophistication hoped that these generalizations would soon dissipate themselves with the advent of the 1960s.

I heard you tell the Negro ministers that the whole thing depended on them. . . . Jesus, man, how do you swallow this! You said afterwards that this was political expediency. Do you think they, the ministers, thought

that? Isn't this merely furthering the thing all intelligent
people are trying to kill?

It is the same with the whole party. When you speak of
civil rights, civil liberties, etc., you think of black vs.
white. When there's talk of investigation of these rights,
of federal grants for education, of cheap housing, in other
words, discrimination, you speak of Negroes. At the Chinese banquet, when all the big whigs got up to talk, they
mentioned first Negroes, and second Chinese. . . . And
that's the way it goes. All America is divided into three
parts: white, black and yellow. . . . How about me?

It doesn't end here. . . . As I said, it sounds petty when
repeated. But when I heard it, when I saw it, it was not.
Obviously, it was not these two examples alone that
caused my decision. The others are too personal to
repeat. They are petty, in the sense that they affected me
because of my sensitivity. I mention three only because
they can be discussed without getting into personalities.

There is no doubt in anyone's mind that is worth consideration that you are the best candidate. Yet you have
found it necessary to tell this only to the non-white community, to spend most of your time in the non-white community, and most of your money. I am against this, practi-
cality be damned! Because this is discrimination and that
is an evil. My life and your life and the life of our society
will not be bothered by the continuance of this method of
political activity.

Surprisingly, his campaign for sheriff did gather re-
spectable grassroots support. "Cockroaches from the barrios

and beaches" began to pass out bumper stickers and lawyers from important organizations, such as the National Lawyers Guild, the ACLU, and some Legal Aid societies were behind him. Soon the news reached higher ranks, up to Gilbert Roland, Vicki Carr, and Anthony Quinn, whom Zeta describes as "those [Chicanos] with red hair and Jewish names." Quinn himself, the most famous Chicano in mainstream America, one who acknowledged and embraced his Mexican roots in public, once introduced Zeta at the Sports Arena on the University of Southern California campus, and later on endorsed his campaign. Zeta rapidly became a celebrity. Salazar covered the overall campaign. His credibility was high. He was invited to parades, delivered speeches, and was frequently interviewed on radio and television. But he never had great expectations. At one point, Salazar asked him at a press conference: "Hey, Buff, what would you do if you actually got elected?" Zeta responded: "I'm just glad I don't have to seriously worry about that."

"Why not, hombre? Maybe you won't win . . . but you're going to get a lot of votes. . . . And that's power."

"What can I do about it?"

"I don't know. . . . All I know is . . . I've heard a lot of talk about you, man. You must know the police are right on your tail. They're just waiting for you to make a mistake."

"So what do you suggest?"

"Just be careful, *viejo*. Be careful. . . . The establishment doesn't like to give power to people like you and me."

In a four-candidate race that included the incumbent, Pete Pritchess, Zeta won some half a million votes. In the *Los Angeles Times,* Salazar wrote that he "was the only little ray of sunshine for the Chicanos." When the last votes were counted, he came in second—not bad for a minority politician. After his defeat, Zeta seemed to undergo another major existential transformation. He was fed up. Once again, he wanted to run away. It was the spring of 1972 and he had given up his legal cases. Many things were unfinished. *Adiós Zeta.* Where to go? He had heard that the Feds from the Department of Treasury were after him. In *The Revolt of the Cockroach People,* his end, unlike the rest, is narrated in the third person. "He didn't know that he'd meet up with Jesus again . . . ," he writes, "or that he'd go on to Ziquítaro and marry a Tarascan princess. He knew his name, yeah, and just a little more. . . . Hell . . . I'm going to write my memoirs before I go totally crazy. Or totally underground." Eventually he decided to cross the border. But his crossing wasn't only physical. It was primarily allegorical. He wanted to return to his Hispanic roots. To become fully Mexican. In letters and conversations, he stated his will to become a south-of-the-border writer. To abandon English, his mother tongue, and switch to his father language: Spanish. He would look for ways to write for mainstream dailies such as *Excélsior* and probably finish a novel.

GUACAMOLE AND DOS EQUIS

Hunter S. Thompson enters the scene. A surviving photograph in the *New York Times* archives has him and Zeta sitting together at the Caesar's Palace bar in Las Vegas. It's 3 A.M. on April 26, 1971, some two weeks after his thirty-sixth birthday. Zeta looks exhausted. He is wearing an expensive lawyer's suit and a flashy tie. His left hand, covered with a black glove, is under his chin. He is drinking Tequila with salt and lemon. Thompson, an admirer of Mohammed Ali and George McGovern, smoking and drinking as well, is more casually dressed: He is wearing glasses, a Safari hat, and sneakers. He also has his left hand under his chin, in a gesture of meditation. Both have a tongue-in-cheek expression: They look serious, professional, but in truth they are totally lost. Their paths crossed when Thompson suggested to his editor at *Rolling Stone* a piece on police brutality in East Los Angeles, which would end up being "Strange Rumblings in Aztlán." The central theme was the death of Rubén Salazar, killed by the LAPD in 1971, at the height of the La Raza movement. According to Paul Perry, author of the 1992 volume *Fear and Loathing: The Strange and Terrible Saga of Hunter S. Thompson*, the gunman was captured later but not arrested, and Salazar had quickly become a legendary martyr. Zeta had met Salazar, recognizable in *The Revolt of the Cockroach People* as Roland Zanzibar, when the journalist interviewed him for KMEX radio station in Los Angeles. He described the encounter in the present tense: "[Salazar] appears relaxed and after a brief conversation I feel that I have his confidence. The talk is warm and friendly and he seems genuinely interested in the subject. It is not simply another day of work for him. He gauges my own sympathies. He knows that the event has great meaning for me. And, from newspaper articles, I know he is regarded as a veteran journalist by his own peers. He has recently returned from Vietnam and has a weekly column in the largest newspaper west of Chicago, the *Los Angeles Times*. Stonewall comes off like an angry baboon in comparison."

Thompson, who appears as the pseudonymous journalist Stonewall in *The Revolt of the Cockroach People,* got details from Zeta. They had met years earlier in Daisy Duck saloon shortly after he moved to Aspen, Colorado, during the summer of 1967. The meeting, at which Bill Kennedy from the *San Juan Star* was also present, was arranged by Mike Solheim, who, according to Peter O. Whitmer, another Thompson biographer, knew them from his days running a bar and coffeehouse in Ketchum, Idaho. According to Perry, Zeta "had been drifting around the country, having had a mental breakdown after his secretary at his Legal Aid job in Oakland died. Fat, plagued by ulcers and searching for the meaning of life, Acosta had had only one legal client, John Tibeau, the actor who had broken his leg in a motorcycle accident with Hunter. Tibeau convinced Acosta to go to Aspen in search of a fellow with a cure for ulcers." Zeta became Thompson's source of information for the East L.A. article, and a friendship developed. "He was the only Mexican lawyer around who specialized in 'Chicano law,'" Thompson told Perry. "Everyone who was pissed at the cops or a landlord wanted to talk to Oscar."

Perry's book devotes a large segment to Zeta. He discusses his upbringing in El Paso and Riverbank, talks about his studies at San Francisco Law School ("the oldest night law school in the state"), his bar examination, and his inferiority complex. Since Zeta was Tibeau's lawyer, his relationship with the self-proclaimed Dr. Gonzo started on a complex note. At one point Zeta asked his friend if he was really a professional writer. The response: "I guess I'm about as much a writer as you are a lawyer." They were surrounded by criminals, alcohol, and psychedelic drugs and were always on a trip. ("I hate to advocate drugs, alcohol, violence, or insanity . . . ," Thompson likes to say, "but they've always worked for me.") While writing the piece, Thompson was struck by the idea of traveling to Las Vegas in search of the American Dream, a sequel to a piece, also for *Rolling Stone*, about the Kentucky Derby. His contact at the magazine, Ralph Steadman, declined, but then a friend at *Sports Illustrated* assigned him to cover the Las Vegas Mint 400 motorcycle race.

A journalist once asked Thompson a few years later: "Did you really have that many drugs?" "Maybe," he answered. "'Fiction is the truest form of journalism.' Faulkner said something like that. You figure it out." Zeta was preparing his defense of the Biltmore 7. Thompson rented a car, which he renamed "the Great Red Shark" and got Zeta to accompany him. The two went wild, and Dr. Gonzo ended up writing a two-thousand-word piece, which *Sports Illustrated* eventually rejected. He then decided to finish the Rubén Salazar story (some nineteen thousand words) and, simultaneously, as Zeta returned to California, he wrote down in his notes every single detail about his and Zeta's excursion into America's wildest face. Every dialogue between Thompson and Zeta was recorded in a portable tape recorder, and the material is still at Hunter's house. He often plays it for visitors and to friends over the phone (as he did to Marco, Zeta's son). In Zeta's circle the certitude remains that Thompson was only marginally the author of *Fear and Loathing in Las Vegas*. According to Peter O. Whitmer's biography, *When the Going Gets Weird,* "when the real-life 300-pound Samoan attorney read the Las Vegas manuscript, he said to editor Alan Rinzler, 'My God! Hunter has stolen my soul! He has taken my best lines and has used me. He has wrung me dry for material.'" Zeta, adds Whitmer, "had a clear dimension of macho black humor in him as well, and a druggie style that was transparent in the book. Regardless, his emotional take on it, he said to Rinzler, was that he felt 'ripped off again.'"

The feud between Thompson and Zeta almost turned nasty but ended up with a fruitful bargain. Zeta was bitter.

He wanted half of the proceeds from *Fear and Loathing in Las Vegas* and a coauthor credit on the cover. According to Perry, he "left his sign, the name ZETA, carved with a knife in the wooden frame of the men's room mirror of the *Rolling Stone* office." While their friendship was in shambles, Zeta threatened to sue Thompson's New York publisher, Random House, for libel, but Rinzler convinced him to sign a waiver stating he would not take action, in trade for giving the Chicano attorney a publishing contract for two of his own books. According to William McKeen, author of a study on Hunter S. Thomspon, Zeta's reaction baffled the publisher's attorneys: "the only thing he objected to was being called 'Samoan.'" Marco Acosta told Whitmer that without the waiver, the book would certainly not have been published. Whitmer adds: "The action in Las Vegas was such a true extension of Oscar Acosta's style in life that when his son read the book, he stated that 'it was hard for me to put the real "crazy" personality of my father in context. I did not see how it was any different from reality. He really was like that. People should not make any mistake; he lived his life with drinking, drugs, music; almost like one constant party. Then he could get up at five in the morning and do a full day's work. . . .'"

The waiver, therefore, was a crucial factor in the making of Zeta's literary career. It's also evidence of his astuteness. Rinzler understood the game well: As an attorney, Zeta knew how to fight in court; interrupting publication of *Fear and Loathing in Las Vegas* would be too costly; a legal battle would take time and money; and if Zeta was indeed the book's coauthor, his obvious talents as a writer could also be shown elsewhere, in a work of his own. And his notoriety as a Robin Hood of the Chicano poor in the Southwest could be a publicity stunt. Zeta, on the other hand, suspected that the Straight Arrow Books contract could well be the only publishing deal of his life. *¡Vato chingón!* After all, no other company was ever interested in his work. Now that his political career was over and his artistic one at an impasse, he saw that taking advantage of his threat to sue Thompson and Rinzler and thus secure a commitment to see his work in print was highly profitable. The waiver was a door to a literary future.

At any rate, the first half of *Fear and Loathing in Las Vegas* was being finished in a frenzy in various hotels when Thompson found out that the National District Attorneys Association's Third Annual Institute on Narcotics and Dangerous Drugs was also in Las Vegas. Since Thompson considered the D.A.s as "brainless thugs," the atmosphere was conducive to explosive, anarchic creativity. "I began writing it during a week of hard typewriter nights in a room at the Ramada Inn—in a place called Arcadia, California. . . . [To relax I would] spend an hour or so, cooling out, by letting my head unwind and my fingers run wild on the big black Selectric . . . jotting down notes about the weird trip to Vegas." But soon he ran out of ideas. So he asked Zeta, at that point way into the Biltmore 7 defense, to join him again in another journey, which he did. As Paul Perry writes, "One night [Thompson's editor] received a phone call from Hunter in Vegas. There was screaming and what sounded like the crashing of dishes in the background, and Hunter seemed beside himself with fear. 'You gotta send money! Oscar is out of control!' shouted Hunter." Thompson's account of the Las Vegas experience was finished six months after the second trip. It opened with an epigraph from Dr. Johnson: "He who makes a beast of himself gets rid of the pain of being a man."

In *Fear and Loathing in Las Vegas,* Thompson comes down as Roul Duke and Zeta as Dr. Gonzo. The book is famous as the ultimate example of so-called gonzo journalism, a most anarchic style of writing which, as Thompson himself once put it in *Playboy,* "involves participating in a story, filling [one's] notebooks with whatever comes up and printing all of it with few if any changes. It produces a very cranked-up style and [one needs to] stay well cranked in order to maintain the pace: Guacamole, Dos Equis and MDA are the staples of [one's] diet." Zeta and Thompson spent "a hell of a time" together in Las Vegas, in what a journalist called "a sixties trip into the seventies." "We took enough speed to keep Hitler awake in the bunker for 50 days," Thompson would write later on, "and enough acid to make him think he was in the Austrian Alps." Zeta is the 300-pound Samoan attorney. Although no full-length description is ever made, Thompson takes every opportunity to portray his companion as a weird, unconventional, minority fellow, sympathetic, drug-addicted, cynical, all of which in his eyes are marvelous qualities. At one point, he tells a boy:

> "I want you to understand that this man at the wheel is my *attorney!* He's not just some dingbat I found on the Strip. Shit, *look* at him! He doesn't look like you or me,

right? That's because he's a foreigner. I think he's probably Samoan. But it doesn't matter, does it? Are you preju-
diced?"

"Oh, hell *no!*" he blurted,

"I didn't think so," I said. "Because in spite of his race,
this man is extremely valuable to me."

Thompson exploited Zeta's dark skin and calls attention
to his attorney's otherness. However, the Samoan reference can easily be traced to Zeta's own work. In his autobiography, he writes that "all my life strangers have been
interested in my ancestry. There is something about my
bearing that cries out for history. I've been mistaken for
American Indian, Spanish, Filipino, Hawaiian, Samoan
and Arabian. No one has ever asked me if I'm a spic or a
greaser. Am I Samoan? Aren't we all? I groan." The nick-
name, nevertheless, pinpoints a crucial dilemma in Zeta's
identity: his looks. As he was growing up in Riverbank, *real*
Mexicans wore long, black patent leather boots and short
pants.

The Roul Duke–Dr. Gonzo relationship inspired a
comic strip, *Fear and Laughter,* produced by Kitchen Sink
Enterprises; one of G. B. Trudeau's *Doonesbury* cartoons;
and a terrible Hollywood film, with Bill Murray playing
Hunter and Peter Boyle as Oscar, called Lazlo in the film,
entitled *Where the Buffalo Roam.* Written by John Kaye,
produced and directed by Art Linson, with music by Neil
Young, and based on Thompson's obituary of Zeta in
Rolling Stone, "The Banshee Screams for Buffalo Meat"
(the producer paid $100,000 for the rights), it was released

in 1980 to largely negative reviews. Roger Angell, in *The New Yorker,* called it "a raunchy comedy." And Merrill Shindler wrote in the *Los Angeles Times*: "The film is, at best, gonzo dreck." As their friendship faded away, Zeta became angry with Thompson because, as he saw it, the gonzo style was their collaborative creation, and his friend had taken all the credit away from him. In a letter to the editor of *Playboy,* dated October 15, 1973, some eight months before his disappearance, he complained:

> Your November issue "On the Scene" section on Mr. Hunter S. Thompson as the creator of Gonzo Journalism, which you say he both created and named. . . . Well, sir, I beg to take issue with you. And with anyone else who says that. In point in fact, Doctor Duke and I—the world-famous Doctor Gonzo—together we both, hand in hand, sought out the teachings and curative powers of the world-famous Savage Henry, the Scag Baron of Las Vegas and in point of fact the term *and* methodology of reporting crucial events under fire and drugs, which are of course essential to any good writing in this age of confusion—all this I say come from out of the mouth of our teacher who is also known by the name of Owl. These matters I point out not as a threat of legalities or etcetera but simply to inform you and to invite serious discussion on the subject.

And he adds that Thompson got the guacamole and Dos Equis from him.

BISON AMERICANUS

As critics have repeatedly stated, his standing in the canon of Latino letters is ambiguous at best, in large part because of his confusing identity. His style is erratic, his language slangy. But his books are living proof of G. K. Chesterton's theory that all slang is metaphor, and all metaphor is poetry. "Sex and race," Zeta once said, "it's one and the same hang up." Joe D. Rodríguez, from San Diego State University, claims that taking to the road is a version of the frontier saga. He also suggests that ethnicity was Zeta's literary mission. He predicts his work will gain momentum in a new generation of readers removed from their ancestral background, yet interested in self-discovery: "The strident militancy in his novels about improving society commands attention. No Chicano author had more enthusiasm for the Chicano cause than Acosta. Both his books often denigrate women and seem not to include them in a Chicano agenda for full rights and equal privileges. Many Chicana . . . critics see his women characters as little more than sources of ego gratification and sexual release. Both books use derogatory labels for ethnics of color and those who happen to be white, which is odd in light of the sensitivity to reverse discrimination shown in Acosta's short story 'Perla Is a Pig.'" Rodríguez adds: "Acosta approaches *Chicanismo* . . . from the angle of the *pocho,* the Latino who speaks English and who has tried to assimilate. Not all Chicanos are immigrants. However, there is an old saying about the third generation of immigrant families needing to explore their roots, and there may be a resurgence of interest in him in the future."

In a letter to Hunter Thompson, with whom, in spite of their enmity, he maintained a dialogue through correspondence, Zeta claimed he wrote his first book "in no more than five weeks of actual time," whereas the second one took him more than twelve. When *The Autobiography of a Brown Buffalo* was published by Straight Arrow Books in October 1972, in hardcover and paperback, it was accompanied by a publicity blurb signaling the public awareness of Zeta's odyssey.

> Oscar Zeta Acosta is best known as the militant Chicano attorney who successfully defended the Biltmore 7 against political and ethnic persecution in the city of Los Angeles. Now he has written his autobiography, the Odyssean quest of a young Mexican-American from a small barrio in Northern California who initially accepts his parents' American Dream to become a varsity athlete, school leader, ace student and government lawyer . . . then rejects the psychic and racial oppression of this life to embark on a series of drug-crazed adventures in San

Francisco, Aspen, and Juarez, returning finally to become Zeta; the world-famous Chicano lawyer who helped to start "the last revolution." The progress of this Decameron-like journey is filled with extraordinary encounters and events, all told in an explosive, madcap, intensely honest, compellingly "good read" style. *Brown Buffalo* makes the debut of a totally original and authentic American literary voice. It is an important book, certain to be required reading in a variety of academic discipline—literature, ethnic studies, sociology, pharmacology. But more importantly, it is an epic of Rabelaisian adventure and excitement.

"I wanted Oscar to be in talk shows," Betty told me during our interview. "He probably needed a publicist, the way famous people have today. Somebody to put you on the air. If Hunter Thompson got all that attention, why didn't Oscar? Perhaps it was the publisher's fault. They didn't promote him. I don't know!" Perhaps. And then again, perhaps not. Not only did the volume seem to have been completed under Thompson's spell, but soon after, he had made peace with the author of *Fear and Loathing in Las Vegas*. To gain acceptance and recognition, he wanted Thompson and his publisher, Alan Rinzler, on his side, not against him. Deep inside, Zeta knew his books were being published not because of their literary value but as a result of a legal deal between him and Straight Arrow Books, one involving Hunter S. Thompson (who, by the way, also ran for the office of sheriff of his respective town, in what he called "a freak power" campaign). Not surprisingly, Zeta's inferiority complex, his second-rateness, bothered him throughout the creative process. Were his literary efforts worth a penny? Would he always remain a shadow? Would he simply make it to literary dictionaries as another one of Hunter's inspirations? "I've cut out the entire Las Vegas thing as such," Zeta writes in a letter to Thompson. "I decided you wouldn't understand it and that others might accuse me of using your book as my notes, etc." He adds: "Perhaps after I write it all out, all of you will come to understand just exactly what you did by coming down to L.A. I think I can make a pretty good argument that it was you, or God through you that called a halt to the bombings. . . . Which means you'll be remembered as the Benedict Arnold of the cockroach revolt."

To his delight, reviews of his autobiography, although scarce, were generally condescending and full of euphemisms. *Choice* wrote: "The sociological and anthropological value of Acosta's life story requires considerable analytical thought to become fully apparent. The book depicts a series of West Coast urban scenes, including vividly described interpersonal encounters between a variety of people in bars, pads, and elsewhere. The language is rich and uninhibited. Not until Chapter 6 does the Chicano lawyer's biography start, but since he dropped his career in Chapter 1 and does not resume it, his future remains, to say the least, in doubt." Similarly, D. R. McDonald, a teacher of creative writing at Stanford University, wrote in the *San Francisco Chronicle* about Zeta's ambiguities: "His narrative shifts back and forth from past to present," he claimed. "He files the City and his drunken cronies at Trader JJ's after quitting as a welfare lawyer. Driving east, his story deeps back into boyhood, and the accounts of his growing up in Riverbank, Ca., are what individualize him. When he jumps back to the present and his escapades through several western towns, I lose interest. The characters—a rich hippie, a paranoid writer, and lesser lights—are not worth the time he kills with them. They are kinky but familiar. Like the Trader JJ's crowd, they see Oscar only as an amiable, hard-drinking Samoan, spic, Aztec, Indian, or whatever he claims to be at the moment. But Oscar himself has never been quite clear where he belongs." The *Saturday Review* argued that "in the end the book is nothing so much as a reflection of Zeta's own solid energy, the drive that earlier saw him through nights of law school and later kept his head afloat while so many around him were throwing off energy like old cloths and sinking in excess."

The first edition of *The Autobiography* had an acknowledgment dated May 1972, in Ziquítaro. It thanked Annie Leibovitz for the cover photograph, as well as his son, his former and current wives, and the *vatos locos* of the Chicano literary magazine *Con Safos*, which published an advance of the text. Zeta signs the acknowledgments, "Chicano Lawyer." Every chapter begins with an illustration of an American bison (*Bison americanus*), which in the 1989 paperback edition is recognized by its scientific name in the dedication page. The volume was followed by Zeta's chronicle of major national and Chicano events in *The Revolt of the Cockroach People,* such as the assassination of Robert Kennedy in 1968 and the Los Angeles Chicano Moratorium in 1970, in which over 30,000 attended a march against the Vietnam War in East L.A. and three people are killed by the police, including Rubén Salazar. Here he metamorphoses into Zeta and assumes the role of *the* Chicano lawyer, a Robin Hood fighting against all odds to defend poor, underrepresented Mexican-Americans. The book opens with the logo of Zeta's campaign for sheriff (used herewith as a frontis piece), and the actual text begins with a rioting scene on December 24, 1969, which Zeta refers to as "Christmas Eve in the year of Huitzilopochtli." We are at St. Basil's Roman Catholic Church, on Wilshire Boulevard, "the richest temple in Los Angeles." It's the apex of the Chicano movement, and there's tension in the air. "It is a night of miracles," wrote Zeta. "Never before have the sons of the conquered *Aztecas* worshipped their dead gods on the doorsteps of the living Christ. While the priests offer red wine and the poor people up-tilt earthen pottery to their brown cold lips, there are tears here, quiet tears of history." After a long period of ambiguity, he feels strong. He knows he is part of the Chicano people—"beautiful people," he writes, with "brown soft skin, purple lips and zoftig [sic] chests." Soon, while the police are waiting outside, the priest asks Chicanos to leave the church.

Although, as John Bruce-Novoa once argued, Zeta, "a Chicano Kerouac," was always "ostracized by the Chicano community as a crazy, drug-taking hippie," he finally acquired the respectability of a professional writer in the early seventies, after *The Autobiography of a Brown Buffalo* was published. Probably unaware of his literary aspirations, many Chicano authors then read him for the first

time and welcomed him as a colleague. Those were years
of narrative explosion, a crucible in which politics and the
arts inspired each other. Edward Hoagland, somewhere in
his 1992 essay collection, *Balancing Acts*, claims that
bursts of enduring literary works of genius often coincide
and follow seminal events in history in which war and revolution occur. The civil rights movement and its Chicano
counterpart did generate an amazing output of literary
material: Rudolfo Anaya's classic *Bless Me, Ultima* was first
published in 1972, followed shortly by Ron Arias's *The
Road to Tamazunchale,* and Rolando Hinojosa Smith's best
installments of the Klail City saga. Those were also the
years of Tomás Rivera's groundbreaking Chicano novel, *Y
no se lo tragó la tierra/And the Earth Did Not Part.* The
literary critic Héctor Calderón suggests a way of approaching Zeta's literary legacy within the context of Mexican-
American letters: His books . . . "should be read as satires,"
he comments. "The satirist can adopt the extreme position
that society is a collection of irrational human beings and
institutions. The satirist uses the free-play of his intellectual wit and fancy to persuade the reader that if anything
can go wrong with society, it already has. If successful, the
satirist will produce in the reader not only amusement, but
also contempt, disgust, and bitterness. Irreverence defines
the tone and attitude of the satirist toward the world.
Satire had nothing to do with the transcendental or the
ideal. . . ." Acosta's satiric vision, "formed out of the sixties
counterculture, focuses on the American ideological solution to the problem of ethnicity, the metaphor of the melt-
ing pot. Acosta's political strategy is to emphasize the eth-

nicity of all his many characters in both rural and urban settings, from Riverbank, California, to San Francisco. Acosta persuades his reader to accept that ethnicity is incompatible with 'American' culture." Calderón concludes that in Zeta's work, "the modern equivalent of the marvelous, the hallucinogens of the sixties drug culture— grass, peyote, cocaine, and acid—are used not to produce any cosmic vision, but to distort and create caricature. That distortion will play a central role" in his books.

Calderón, it seems to me, overrates Zeta's oeuvre. While the Brown Buffalo might indeed be a satirist, the literary critic portrays him as a writer fully conscious, in control of his craft. The opposite is true. As reviewer Arthur Ramírez, considerably more up front about Zeta's talent, once wrote: he "has his faults. . . . At times he might be trivial and trite, banal and boring (rarely) . . . undisciplined, unrestrained and digressive, self-indulgent and unoriginal in both subject matter and style, his language lacking polish, his structure rather formless." Zeta used the art of writing both as therapy and as escape. He embellished his past, he reinvented his persona, all in search of a more adequate place in society. Furthermore, he reminds me of Piri Thomas, the Puerto Rican author of *Down These Mean Streets,* another autobiographical product of the sixties, this one about Spanish Harlem. At the beginning of his book, Thomas finds himself standing alone on a roof and looking at New York City. "Hey, World, here I am," he writes. "Hallo, World—this is Piri. That's me. I wanna tell ya I'm here . . . and I want recognition." Zeta also strives for recognition, for acknowledgment. Not only does he want to be accepted, he is anxious to become the center of attention.

Zeta's growing if evasive prestige among Chicano intellectuals materialized into readings, academic invitations, and literary speeches. In August 1972, David F. Gómez asked him to write a ten-to-twelve-page foreword to a new book on Chicanos in East Los Angeles, which Beacon Press, in Boston, planned to publish in spring 1973, complete with photographs of people and scenes of the barrio. The title was *Somos Chicanos: Strangers in Our Own Land,* and the volume would offer an unsophisticated account of the Mexican-American struggle of resistance and liberation. Zeta agreed, but never a methodical professional, he failed to keep his promise. Nevertheless, he is mentioned a couple of times in the book, once about his impromptu defense of Rubén Salazar on September 29, 1970, the other about Zeta's legal challenge of racial exclusion in the selection of jurors for the Los Angeles County grand jury, also in 1970.

Half a decade after his disappearance, critic John Bruce-Novoa described him as a believer in the American Dream, "having lived according to its clichés all his life." His political flight, he stated, must "be read as the failure of the 1960s' ideal of the grand coalitions." Most of his Chicano peers met him in the fall of 1973, at an artistic event held at the University of Southern California, called Floricanto, a series that went on throughout the years. Rolando Hinojosa-Smith recalls:

It was a very well organized and coordinated affair; each of us read from our works and many of us there met for the very first time. For example, as Tomás Rivera and I were chatting away, Ron Arias came up and introduced

himself to us. His *Tamazunchale* was still in the manuscript
stage. [We] met other writers as well: Sergio Elizondo
and the poets Lin Romero and Verónica Chamberlain,
among others. . . . Meeting Zeta here was a bonus . . .
(I'm not too sure if people called him Oscar; as I recall,
when either speaking of him or about him, Zeta was the
name used.) . . . I'd taught *Brown Buffalo* that same year
and one of the organizers had given me a hardback copy
of *Cockroach* on the previous night. I figured, given the
man's energy and vitality, that he'd written more than
we'd seen at the time. I found him warm, giving, and
approachable. I must imagine he had an ego as all people
do, but it wasn't in evidence during the conference. What
I did see was an openness and a warm smile. I also saw he
was a man of great humor, *ocurrente* as we say in Spanish.
No malice in his humor, though.

Hinojosa-Smith remembers him as a big-chested man.
As recalled by attendees, Zeta's reading was a hit. (There is
a video of it.) He wore a white A-line undershirt as distinct
from the usual T. He read the chapter about the autopsy.
He allowed the material to speak for itself: no histrionics.
Hinojosa Smith saw him as an agent of transmission, with a
powerful, convincing voice. Hinojosa Smith admired his
literary output, his wit, satire, and irony. "He possessed
and managed those three different forms of humor to a
high degree. Too, there was so little humor in those days,
and then to read a seemingly, but only seemingly, reckless,
carefree style made me not only laugh aloud but also made
me realize that here was a daring writer. No, there was

nothing safe about the man at all." He adds: "The success of his two books had not gone to his head, I don't think. The other writers, the older as well as the younger ones, admired him for his work, and it was generally accepted that he would continue to produce as time went by. This was a given; there was no question as to his ability."

Raúl R. Salinas, a native from San Antonio, the Chicano poet responsible for *Un Trip Through the Mind* who had been in jail on and off from 1958 to 1972, also met Zeta at the Floricanto reunion and took some photographs, now in the archives at Stanford University. He recalls:

> People addressed him in various ways: Oscar, Brown Buffalo, Zeta. . . . He was a very important person: an optimist, a dreamer, always encouraging things to change. But like most of us, his talent was exploited by the Anglo establishment. In his case it was Hunter Thompson. That guy stole Brown Buffalo's gonzo style, he turned it into mass-production merchandise. . . . And yet, he had many enemies. Some Chicanas detested him. I remember some of them in San Diego telling me, 'This *vato* is grouse!' A sexist, they said. They thoroughly disliked his treatment of women in *The Autobiography of a Brown Buffalo.* . . . Is he a hero? A myth? Who knows him? I guess it depends on who you ask. The older Chicano generation has a deep affection for Brown Buffalo, but young people know very little, if anything, about him. *¿Sabes?* they know almost nothing about *el movimiento.* I am sure the closer you get to Los Angeles, the stronger the memory. . . .

During a trip to San Antonio, I called Sandra Cisneros, the feminist Chicana writer responsible for *Woman Hollering Creek and Other Stories* and *The House on Mango Street,* to get her opinion of Zeta. She was washing her hair when I asked her about Zeta. "What am I going to tell you, Ilan? *Tu sabes,* I really have nothing to say. I have his books, sure. But I've never read them, not entirely. His writing never spoke to me. I never found anything to identify with in them." I inquired about Zeta's feminine fetishism. "I don't know," she replied. "That's an ongoing problem with Chicano letters. I guess I would only read him if I was in jail!" Rudolfo Anaya, another classic Chicano writer, never met him. "I read his work when it first came out," he writes in his correspondence, "and even taught it in my Chicano literature classes. The students like *The Revolt of the Cockroach People,* but had a harder time with his other book even though it spoke to the problem of lost identity. Zeta put a different slant, a zing, to our literature, and the tragedy of his disappearance is that it cut short his development. He had a lot to share, and it was cut short."

MAY MY WRATH
ABIDE FOREVER

Among the most interesting items in Zeta's archives at UCSB is a sixty-minute, black-and-white VHS video probably filmed on September 16, 1972, at the home of Robert Henry, a friend of Zeta's. Originally meant as an interview by a friend to support the publicity campaign of *The Autobiography of a Brown Buffalo,* it is utterly worthless in terms of promotion. In a ten-minute segment, Zeta reads from his book. What the video does do is shed light on his daily domestic conduct. The camera never moves, only the lens zooms or opens up to enlarge the visual frame. Most of the time Zeta is sitting at the table, Marco at his side, while some friends (Robert and Ann Henry, Irwin Segal, and Ron McClure) come and go. They smoke pot and Zeta offers some to his son, but then hesitates while making a joke about morality. The conversation wanders without direction. Nothing is really said, nothing is worth remembering. In the viewer's mind, the picture that emerges is one of sadness and confusion: the paternal figure, a self-possessed brat, simultaneously feared and admired, is the center of gravity. But Zeta's attitude only contributes to a state of general disorder, for Zeta was a consummate master of disarray and entanglement.

In the fall of that year Zeta was living at the apartment of his maternal aunt Jossie. He was last seen by peers and family at a Thanksgiving party in November 1973 at his sister Anita Acosta's house. They all had a good time. As usual, Zeta was obese, angry, and outspoken. At age thirty-nine, he had numerous plans for the future. In spite of his serious drug addiction, he would exercise regularly, and Marco remembers him swimming shortly after the party. That is also the last time he saw his father. Shortly thereafter, Zeta had an ulcer attack and was hospitalized at John Wesley Hospital in San Francisco for over a week. Around January 1974, his mother, Marco's grandmother, visited him. He said he planned to go to Mexico. He was ready to embark on another book. Next thing, he was in Mazatlán. Marco is sure his father was involved in drug trafficking. He wanted to make a quick buck and was dealing with a group of lords in Mexicali and Morelia. A friend of the family, Irwin Segal, was with Zeta in Mexico and has confirmed the fact to Marco and others. Supposedly, Zeta died at a shoot-out after an argument that turned sour. A second possibility is that he was on a boat on his way to Puerto Vallarta and then Santa Cruz, California, when a storm hit. In any event, his body was never found. And a third likelihood is that, as a result of his drug and alcohol addiction, his ulcers, and psychological breakdowns, he simply had a heart attack—*un ataque fatídico.* Marco and

Betty talked to him in June 1974. He implied he was about to make a lot of money and would be back in the fall. Nobody ever heard from him again.

His renewal and ultimate disappearance, of course, invoke the last days of the Civil War writer Ambrose Bierce, who, during the 1910 revolution, also vanished after crossing the U.S.-Mexico border. (Carlos Fuentes has a short novel about him: *Old Gringo*.) The other side emerges as a pit in which American men of genius are swollen. And Zeta's linguistic switch brings to mind the oeuvre of José Antonio Villarreal, the so-called father of Chicano fiction, whose autobiographical narrative, *Pocho*, published in 1959, is widely and mistakenly considered the very first Mexican-American novel. Villarreal, the son of a revolutionary soldier and migrant worker from Mexico, after writing in English, decided to give up his United States residence and move down to Mexico. His journey was perceived as symbolic: a return, much like Zeta's a decade later. Through his novels, Zeta always shows signs of being troubled for having given up Spanish and because, as he put it, "I tried so hard to be accepted by whites." He finally realized he was neither a Mexican nor an Anglo-American, but an artifice. Would the reality south of the Rio Grande allow him to see his face better in the mirror, to come to terms with his duality?

According to Paul Perry, after *Rolling Stone* moved to New York in 1977, hospital bills with "Oscar Zeta Acosta" on them started showing up in their accounting department. One was for a broken arm. Inquiries were made to track them down, to no avail. But the last pieces of correspondence available at UCSB are from the early months of 1974. He wants to travel to Mazatlán, where he will try to relax as much as his character will allow. From John Wesley Hospital, in Los Angeles, on January 13, he wrote to his son telling him of his plans to write another novel, *The Rise and Fall of General Z.* He also sends him a handwritten will, the second Zeta would ever draft in secret. It's obvious he understood *el final* was imminent. Otherwise, why write a testament? Was he involved in a drug cartel? Did he fear for his life? He doesn't explain to Marco why he has been hospitalized. He was dreaming of going to *el Distrito Federal,* Mexico's capital, but things have changed. A segment of the text reads: "Chooch, Just in case, I thought you'd better hang on to this. It is a legal will. I expect I'll be worth a million by the time the grim reaper comes for me. Put it in a safe deposit. I'll be out of the hospital this week. I'll let you know where I end up. Probably with Annie and Martha. . . . I got myself an agent, Helen Brann of New York, and Random House is interested in my next book. . . . Don't forget, keep your socks up and your toes dry. Your only father, Oscar."

Then comes his "Last Will and Testament of Oscar Acosta" (notice now: the "Zeta" has been dropped), signed by a "Chicano Lawyer." It states:

> I, Oscar Acosta, being of sound mind hereby declare: I revoke all former wills, and specifically the one of December 1973 in which I bequeathed the major portion of my estate to my former spouse; I bequeath and devise and dispose and give all of my estate, all my earthly

belongings, both real and personal, choices in action, accounts receivable, and all royalties from all my publications, all memorabilia, files and unpublished works, in short: everything that I possess at the time of my death is for my only son, Marco F. M. Acosta. If any person should contest this will or make any attempt to share in the proceeds of my estate, to that person I give ten dollars and may my wrath abide in her forever. I suggest that Neil Herring, Esq., of Los Angeles County, be appointed administrator of my estate.

The strongest explanation for Zeta's disappearance, writes Joe Rodríguez, has to do with paranoia and narcotics. "Drugs may have intensified his feeling about going off the deep end. . . . Acosta lived in an 'as if' world because he did not have one definition of himself or a singular sense of who he was." In 1986, more than a decade after Zeta's presumed death, Neil Herring would decline the suggestion, and in the mid-eighties, Marco Acosta would file a petition to remain sole owner and administrator of his father's estate. He conducted a relentless search for Zeta, one that lasted several years. He wrote to the U.S. Coast Guard and the Federal Bureau of Investigation, among other government institutions, as well as to the Salvation Army, describing his father as "a missing person." His grandfather Manuel, Zeta's dad, also wrote a few letters, and Zeta's oldest sister, Marta, from Los Angeles, even traveled to Mazatlán to search for him.

His sister Anita, now also a novelist, has a completely different theory. She is certain that agents of the U.S. gov-

ernment disposed of him. "They used to come knocking at
my door when Oscar was living with me," she told me.
"They wanted to get rid of him. They wanted him to disappear." She believes they tracked him down and is confident
that his death was political. It's hard not to think of his disappearance in theological terms: like Jesus Christ, Zeta was
betrayed and crucified by an untrustworthy environment.
He sold others the idea that his earthly existence was the
embodiment of suffering, other people's suffering. A
sojourner, a time bomb, an explosive man of the sixties, a
lost soul, his spirit still wanders. He was a paranoid who
saw himself as a messiah. His fame as a Los Angeles attorney made him insecure. He was sure government forces
were out to get him. He had a vision of doom regarding
the Chicano movement. He was sure state officials had
infiltrated it and delivered secret messages to the FBI.
And yet, he once again dreamed of being the Hispanic
Mahatma Gandhi.

The FBI file includes information gathered between
1970 and 1973 documenting Zeta's political activities. He is
listed as participating in "civil disturbances, anti-U.S.
demonstrations or hostile incidents," and using "threaten-
ing or abusive statements about the U.S. or foreign officials." Apparently, informants within the Chicano movement kept delivering updates on Zeta's behavior. The file
was finally closed on December 11, 1973, but the reasons
listed were censored out of the file, leaving very little
information other than that there was "no information of
current revolutionary activities." When Marco Acosta con-
tacted the FBI, no further details were given to him.

At the end of *The Autobiography of a Brown Buffalo,* Zeta writes of his future plans. He will become a true leader. He will be immortal. His secret goal has been to secede, to push Mexican-Americans to a showdown with the Anglo establishment, which will end in the creation of a new state, Aztlán, in the Southwest. He will be the leader in its shaping, although not its president. His dream is to start the revolution, not to lead it once its objectives have been achieved. And yet, he fools himself. He claims he doesn't want to lead anyone. He would rather be alone.

I have [now] devised a plan, straightened out the philosophy and set up the organization. When I have the one million Brown Buffaloes on my side I will present the demands for a new nation to both the U.S. Government and the United Nations . . . and then I'll split and write the book. I have no desire to be a politician. I don't want to lead anyone. I have no practical ego. I am not ambitious. I merely want to do what is right. Once in every century there comes a man who is chosen to speak for his people. Moses, Mao and Martin are examples. Who's to say that I am not such a man? In this day and age the man for all seasons needs many voices. Perhaps that is why the gods have sent me into Riverbank, Panama, San Francisco, Aspen and Juarez. Perhaps that is why I've been taught so many trades. Who will deny that I am unique?

Obviously he had a tendency to inflate his own stature. As a writer, his work stands not on its artistic merit but because of its ideological echoes. He died without a national prominence equal to that of major Chicano leaders like César Chávez or martyrs like the journalist Rubén Salazar. And yet, his actions and written legacy are a testament to an entire era and a complex ethnic experience. Indeed, his life and his work *were* the Chicano experience—larger than life, exaggerated. He personifies the alienation, disdain, insecurity, oppression, the whole love-hate relationship of Chicanos to America. He remains a symbol of his people's agony and energy, hope and despair. A leader with too much of an inferiority complex. *A Zeta no se lo llevó la chingada. . . . ¡Claro que no!* A role model who often lost control of his impulses. When I asked many Chicano activists and artists about Zeta, they uniformly, symphonically described his legacy as one of hope. "He showed us hope," said one. To which a second added: "He showed that once we can use the language of our oppressors, we can become part of the system, and change it from within. He proved that the struggle can be fought on new, different fronts. That one can write a book that speaks to many readers and whose message will not die in spite of time passing by." To do what's right. . . . Should we expect Zeta's Second Coming? His last written words to his son resonate in my mind: "Don't forget, keep your socks up and your toes dry. . . ."

Take one last look at his crude facial gesture in the Annie Leibovitz photo: the Bronze Superman, aka the Brown Buffalo—the ultimate *desaparecido,* the king of excess.

Yeah, *vato.* Don't forget!

CHRONOLOGY

1935 Oscar Acosta is born on April 8 in El Paso, Texas.

1940 The Acosta family moves to Riverbank, now part of Modesto, California.

1942 The Sleepy Lagoon Incident takes place in Los Angeles, in which twenty-four Chicano youths are charged with gang killings; seventeen are sentenced to prison until their convictions are reversed for lack of evidence and for civil rights violations.

1943 The Zoot Suit Riots, in which U.S. servicemen attack Chicanos, occur in Los Angeles, San Diego, Philadelphia, Chicago, and Detroit.

1949–52 Zeta attends Oakdale Joint Union High School. He has his first romance and soon becomes a fervent Baptist. He rejects a music scholarship to the University of Southern California, enlists in the United States Air Force, and is shipped to Panama, turning into a minister at a lepers' colony.

1956 As Operation Wetback, in which more than two million Mexicans have been deported in three years, is terminated, Zeta is honorably discharged from the air force. He tries to commit suicide in New Orleans. Shortly after, he marries Betty Daves, whom he met at a Modesto hospital.

1957   He begins a ten-year-long psychiatric treatment.

1959   His son, Marco Federico, is born. Soon after, Zeta suffers another mental breakdown. José Antonio Villarreal publishes *Pocho,* considered to be the first Chicano novel in English.

1962–67 The National Farm Workers Association is founded in Delano, California, by César Chávez and Dolores Huerta. Zeta divorces Betty Daves. He begins sending out manuscripts to New York publishers. Writes poetry, a two-act play, and some short stories, only one of which, "Perla Is a Pig," is accepted for publication. He begins studying law at night at San Francisco Law School, passes the California State Bar Exam in his second try, and becomes an attorney for the East Oakland Legal Aid Society, an antipoverty agency near Modesto. In 1966 César Chávez and Dolores Huerta lead farm workers on a three-hundred-mile march from Delano to Sacramento, California. Rodolfo "Corky" González founds the Crusade for Social Justice in Denver, Colorado. At the end of this time period Zeta quits his Oakland legal job.

1967   Zeta travels by car around the Southwest. Reies López Tijerina and his supporters storm a courtroom in Tierra Amarilla, New Mexico, to free colleagues held as political prisoners. "Corky" González publishes his militant poem *Yo Soy Joaquín / I Am Joaquín.*

1968   César Chávez begins the first of many fasts to protest violence. Robert F. Kennedy is assassinated in Los

Angeles, California. Zeta is put in a jail in Ciudad
Juárez, Mexico. He arrives in California and acquires
a new identity, becoming Buffalo Z. Brown. He
meets César Chávez, Angela Davis, Rodolfo "Corky"
González, and other Chicano and civil rights activists.
He represents poor Chicanos in East Los Angeles,
becomes a vociferous lawyer, and challenges racial
exclusion on the California Grand Jury. Chicano
teachers boycott and walk out of schools, and nearly
3,500 students stay away from classes for eight days.

1969   Protesting Chicano fatalities in Vietnam, the Brown
Berets organize the National Chicano Moratorium
Committee in Los Angeles. The La Raza Unida party
is formed in Crystal City, Texas, under the leadership
of José Angel Gutiérrez. Zeta meets his second wife,
Socorro Aguiniga. His legal work and militant activi-
ties continue. He takes part in the St. Basil's Roman
Catholic Church riot.

1970   Zeta defends Mexican-Americans charged with setting fires at the Biltmore Hotel in Los Angeles while
Governor Ronald Reagan delivered a speech. He
declares his candidacy for sheriff of Los Angeles
County as a La Raza Unida party independent, running with an anarchist, apocalyptic platform that
promises to abolish the police force. He is interviewed by Rubén Salazar for KMEX radio. The La
Raza Unida party becomes a national independent
party, with *El plan espiritual de Aztlán* as its platform. Over 30,000 attend the National Chicano
Moratorium march in East Los Angeles against the
Vietnam War. Three people are killed by the police,
including *Los Angeles Times* reporter Rubén Salazar.
The United Farm Workers Union signs contracts
with California grape growers.

1971   Reies López Tijerina is paroled after serving three years in prison for storming a courthouse in Tierra Amarilla. Tomás Rivera's *Y no se lo tragó la tierra / And the Earth Did Not Part* wins an award and is quickly considered a Chicano literary classic. Disappointed with his career, Zeta gives up the practice of law. Soon after, he is arrested on charges for possession of drugs. After meeting Hunter S. Thompson in the summer of 1967, he travels with him to Las Vegas. He divorces his second wife.

1972   Publication of *The Autobiography of a Brown Buffalo* by Oscar "Zeta" Acosta, as well as *Bless Me Ultima* by Rudolfo Anaya and Rodolfo Acuña's *Occupied America: A History of Chicanos.* Rumors circulate that the FBI is after Zeta for political activism.

1973   Publication of *The Revolt of the Cockroach People.* He is last seen by his family at Thanksgiving.

1974   He is hospitalized for ulcer attacks in San Francisco. In June, Oscar "Zeta" Acosta disappears in Mazatlán, Mexico, and is never seen again. A year later, the United States officially ends its military involvement in Vietnam.

SELECTED
BIBLIOGRAPHY

Acosta, Oscar "Zeta." "The Autobiography of a Brown Buffalo," *Con Safos* 2, no. 7 (1971): 34–46.

———. *The Autobiography of a Brown Buffalo*. San Francisco: Straight Arrow Books, 1972; reprint. New York: Vintage, 1989.

———. "The Autobiography of a Brown Buffalo," in *Growing Up Latino: Memoirs and Stories*, edited by Harold Augenbraum and Ilan Stavans. Boston: Houghton Mifflin, 1993: 193–207.

———. "Perla Is a Pig," *Con Safos* 2, no. 5 (1970): 5–14; reprinted in *Voices of Aztlán: Chicano Literature Today*, edited by Dorothy E. Harth and Lewis M. Baldwin. New York: Mentor, 1974: 28–48.

———. "The Revolt of the Cockroach People," *La Gente* (November–December 1973): 4–5, 12.

———. *The Revolt of the Cockroach People*. San Francisco: Straight Arrow Books, 1973; reprint. New York: Vintage, 1989.

———. "Tres Cartas de Zeta," *Con Safos* 2, no. 6 (1970): 29–31.

Acuña, Rodolfo. *Occupied America: A History of Chicanos*. 3rd ed. New York: HarperCollins, 1988.

Alurista. "Alienación e ironía en los personajes de Arlt y Acosta," *Grito del Sol* 2, no. 4 (1977): 69–80.

———. *Oscar Zeta Acosta: In Context*, Ph.D. Dissertation, Ann Arbor, MI, 1983.

Blazer, Sam. "Review of *The Revolt of the Cockroach People*," *The Nation* (13 April 1974): 469–71.

Bruce-Novoa, John. "Fear and Loathing on the Buffalo Trail," *MELUS* 6, no. 4 (1979): 39–50.

Calderón, Héctor. *Criticism in the Borderlands: Studies in Chicano Literature, Culture, and Ideology.* Durham: Duke University Press, 1991.

———. "To Read Chicano Narrative: Commentary and Metacommentary," *Mester* (1983): 3–14.

———, and Ramón Saldívar, eds. *Chicano Criticism in Social Context.* Durham: Duke University Press, 1989.

Cárdenas de Dwyer, Carlota. "Chicano Literature 1965–1975: The Flowering of the Southwest." Ph.D. Dissertation, Ann Arbor, MI, 1974.

Carroll, E. Jean. *Hunter. The Strange and Savage Life of Hunter S. Thompson.* New York: Dutton, 1993.

Choice 10 (May 1973): 538.

Eger, Ernestin N., ed. *A Bibliography of Criticism of Contemporary Chicano Literature.* Berkeley: Chicano Studies Library Publication, 1980.

Felton, David. "When the Weird Turn Pro," *Rolling Stone* magazine (29 May 1980): 39.

Grajeda, Rafael. "The Figure of the Pocho in Contemporary Chicano Fiction." Ph.D. Dissertation, Ann Arbor, MI, 1974.

Hernández, Guillermo. *Chicano Satire: A Study in Literary Culture.* Austin, Tex.: University of Texas Press, 1991.

Kanon, Joseph. Review of *The Autobiography of a Brown Buffalo, Saturday Review* (11 November 1972): 68–69.

Kawalczyk, Kimberly A. "Oscar Zeta Acosta: The Brown Buffalo and His Search for Identity," *Americas Review* 19, nos. 3–4 (1989): 199–209.

Leal, Luis. "Mexican American Literature: A Historical Perspective," *Revista Chicano-Riqueña* 1, no. 1 (1973): 32–44.

———, with Fernando de Necochea, Francisco Lomelí, and Roberto G. Trujillo, eds. *A Decade of Chicano Literature (1970–1979): Critical Essays and Bibliography.* Santa Barbara, California: Editorial La Causa, 1982.

Padilla, Genaro M. *The Progression from Individual to Social Consciousness in Two Chicano Novels: José Antonio Villarreal and Oscar Zeta Acosta,* Ph.D. Dissertation, Ann Arbor, MI, 1992.

———. "The Self as Cultural Metaphor in Acosta's *Autobiography of a Brown Buffalo,*" *Journal of General Education* 35, no. 1 (1994): 242–59.

Paredes, Raymund A. "Los Angeles from the Barrio: Oscar Zeta Acosta's *The Revolt of the Cockroach People,*" in *Los Angeles in Fiction,* David Fine, ed. Albuquerque: University of New Mexico Press, 1984: 209–22.

Pettit, Arthur G. *Images of the Mexican American in Fiction and Film.* Edited with an afterword by Dennis S. Showalter. College Station, TX: Texas A&M University Press, 1980.

Perry, Paul. *Fear and Loathing: The Strange and Terrible Saga of Hunter S. Thompson.* New York: Thunder's Mouth Press, 1992.

Ramírez, Arthur. Review of *The Autobiography of a Brown Buffalo. Revista Chicano-Riqueña* 3, no. 3 (1975): 85.

Rivera, Tomás. "Into the Labyrinth: The Chicano in Literature," *Southwestern American Literature* 2, no. 2 (1973): 90–97.

Robinson, Cecil. *Mexico and the Hispanic Southwest in American Literature.* Tucson: University of Arizona Press, 1977.

Rodríguez, Joe D. "The Chicano Novel and the North American Narrative of Survival," *Denver Quarterly* 16 (Fall 1981): 229–35.

———. "God's Silence and the Shrill of Ethnicity in the Chicano Novel," *Explorations in Ethnic Studies* 4 (July 1981): 14–21.

————. "Oscar Zeta Acosta," *Dictionary of Literary Biography* vol. 82. Detroit, Mich.: Gale Research, 1981: 3–10.

————. "The Sense of Mestizaje in Two Latino Novels," *Revista Chicano-Riqueña* 12 (Spring 1984): 57–63.

Romero, Oswaldo. Review of *The Autobiography of a Brown Buffalo, Mester* 4, no. 2 (1974): 141.

Saldívar, Ramón. "A Dialectic of Difference: Toward a Theory of the Chicano Novel," *MELUS* 6, no. 3 (1979): 78–89.

Shular, Antonia, Tomás Ybarra-Frausto, and Joseph Sommers, eds. *Literatura chicana: Texto y contexto/Chicano Literature: Text and Context.* Englewood Cliffs, NJ: Prentice-Hall, 1972.

Simmen, Edward. *The Chicano: From Caricature to Self-Portrait.* New York: Mentor Books, 1971.

Smith, Norman D. "Buffalos and Cockroaches: Acosta's Siege at Aztlán," *Latin American Literary Review* 5, no. 10 (1977): 85–97.

Sommer, Joseph, and Tomás Ybarra-Frausto, eds. *Modern Chicano Writers: A Collection of Critical Essays.* Englewood Cliffs, NJ: Prentice-Hall, 1979.

Somoza, Oscar Urquídez. "Visión axiológica en la narrativa chicana." Ph.D. Dissertation, Ann Arbor, MI, 1977.

Stavans, Ilan. "*Bandido Vendido*: The Life & Times of Oscar Zeta Acosta," *Bloomsbury Review* (January–February 1992): 4.

————. *The Hispanic Condition: Reflections on Culture and Identity in America.* New York: HarperCollins, 1995.

————. "The Latin Phallus," *Transition* 65 (Spring 1995): 48–68.

Steadman, Ralph. "Gonzo Goes to Holywood: The Strange and Terrible Saga of *Where the Buffalo Roam,*" *Rolling Stone* magazine (29 May 1980): 38–40.

Thompson, Hunter S. "Fear and Loathing in the Graveyard of the Weird: The Banshee Screams for Buffalo Meat," *Rolling Stone* magazine (15 December 1977); anthologized in *The Great Shark Hunt: Strange Tales from a Strange Time; Gonzo Papers, vol 1.* New York: Summit Books, 1979: 495–516.

————. *Fear and Loathing in Las Vegas*. New York: Random House, 1971; reprint. Vintage, 1989.

————. "Strange Rumblings in Aztlán," *Rolling Stone* magazine (29 April 1971); anthologized in *The Great Shark Hunt*. New York: Summit Books, 1979: 119–51.

Thwaitasn, Joanna. "The Uses of Irony in Oscar Zeta Acosta's *Autobiography of a Brown Buffalo*," *Americas Review* 20, no. 1 (1992): 73–92.

Whitmer, Peter O. *When the Going Gets Weird: The Twisted Life and Times of Hunter S. Thompso: A Very Unauthorized Biography*. New York: Hyperion, 1993.

INDEX

142   I N D E X

Ilan Stavans is a novelist and critic born in 1961. His books include *Growing Up Latino, The Hispanic Condition,* and *Tropical Synagogues.* The recipient of a National Endowment for the Humanities grant, the Latino Literature Prize, and other awards, he teaches at Amherst College in Massachusetts.